SHAMELESS SVENGALI

*101 Questions Americans Need
Trump to Answer HONESTLY!*

"*Keen observations of a man's character are often more reliable indicators of the facts than any version of truth a Svengali might try to peddle.*"

-- Karen Ann Carpenter

SHAMELESS SVENGALI

101 Questions Americans Need Trump
to Answer HONESTLY!

To the American People

God Help us all

INTRODUCTION

This book is in the form of 101 questions to Donald J. Trump. These are all questions that, if asked directly, Trump would not likely answer honestly.

That leaves us, the American people, struggling to decipher the facts about Trump. Every question in this book has either an explanation or a definite answer. Explanations are provided as background material on the questions themselves. Through reported material, we have also answered (to the best of our ability) many of the 101 questions throughout this book. Trump unknowingly answered some of the questions himself -- through his direct quotes.

Imagine for a moment we *could* trust Trump to clarify these questions accurately. All right, it will take you more than a minute to get to *that* frame of mind, but *try*. Honest answers would expose much of what goes on inside this man's skull, and what is happening in and to our country.

In that spirit, we call upon Donald J. Trump to resolve any or all of these 101 questions HONESTLY for us. It would delight us to give him the opportunity to provide his own answers, neatly arranged beneath ours, in an amended version of this text.

Awhhhhh . . . what the heck, the guy *is* president, we'll put his responses *before* ours!

But they must be *provable*, straightforward answers.

Otherwise, our remarks will stand.

Some questions are just for fun, others we desperately deserve to have answered for us, and far too many are urgent queries. How much harm is Trump inflicting upon our country and its outstanding citizens with his continual deception?

We should all be deeply afraid.

We'll start off easy with fun inquiries in the section -- *Just Because*. Then we'll head into alternative subjects -- *Random Events, Delusional, A Marriage Made in Heaven*, etc.

And then . . . well, there's really no end to it all, but we'll finish this book with questions that could prove -- *Dangerous and Scary*.

All the information in this book is about situations that occurred BEFORE the mid-term elections (with a special section about Trump's ridiculous threats and promises before that election).

Since things change rapidly in Trump World, please keep in mind that all of these questions are snapshots of moments in time. You'll likely spot a mention of a "current" cabinet member who has already left Trump's Administration. The discrepancies about Trump's wall were recorded before the government shutdown, before Trump hijacked congress and threatened to proclaim a national emergency and/or divert funds from disaster victims to get his way. Fluctuating gas prices might be up or down at the time of your reading, but at the time of the writing, prices *were* on their way up. Mentions of increased immigration were written during a time of a massive influx of immigrants, (a number that is ever-fluctuating). Overall, migration is way down from peak levels of years ago.

So keep in mind that each question describes a point of time in Trump World, not the overall, constantly emerging big picture.

SHAMELESS SVENGALI

Trump loves to dispense nicknames, so we've got one for him: Shameless Svengali.

Heck, it could be a lot worse . . .

We're being soft on him.

It's clear that The Shameless Svengali has two purposes in his world.

- **To make as much money as feasible, by any means necessary.**
- **To be the all-powerful king.**

True, one *could* argue that Trump does have other goals in life, like cheating on his wives with as many gorgeous babes as possible. Or exacting as much brutal revenge on his perceived enemies as possible. But actions like that really just fall into a sub-category of being the king. So, for simplicity sake, we'll concentrate on Trump's two primary aspirations in life, under which we believe, all his other motivations fall.

- **Money**
- **King**

Money: Trump has run every con in the book to shift funds from other people's pockets into his. He's taken money from daddy. He's cheated his employees and dropped *their* hard-earned cash into *his* already bulging pockets. He's sold real estate under fraudulent pretexts. He's hit up everyone imaginable for money, from his family to banks to foreign powers . . .

He's worked every conceivable loophole to dodge paying his fair share of taxes. He's allegedly used his family's various foundations to shift donor contributions into his businesses. There is also every indication that Trump is no stranger to the art of real estate money-laundering, or that he had Russian partners. Nowadays, Trump makes even more money from his powerful position and has worked out numerous new approaches in screwing the American taxpayers.

King: Trump has always needed to be the boss. But that craving has morphed into an obsession to be king. He would prize nothing more than to be an absolute autocrat, with ultimate authority over all of us.

But our overindulged Shameless Svengali smacked into a big beautiful concrete wall. Being a monarch in America doesn't come as readily as other lifelong privileges he's taken for granted. It's easy to recognize the esteem and jealousy Trump feels toward the world's dictators. The total dictatorial authority our Shameless Svengali craves is much more readily secured in other parts of the world.

For example, Kim Jong Un, the leader of North Korea, murders anyone he feels might be a threat to his ultimate authority -- even if they're his own relatives. If any of the leader's subjects show the slightest distaste for the regime, Kim Jong Un throws them into prison/work camps and brutalizes them. This is a harrowing death sentence for most of these captives, and often for their families as well.

Easy, peasy, *right*?

With looming threats like those, you won't find very many resistors organizing protest marches against the government.

But Trump can't threaten us with those same fear-mongering tactics. The American people have long been blessed to live in a land where despots can't bully and control us. Our forefathers, who believed King George III was a mad tyrant, set up the government of the United States with checks and balances so that an oppressor like George could never rule over them again. They intended to protect all future Americans from authoritarians as well with their brilliant, painstakingly implemented form of government.

And it's worked!

So far . . .

But current day scholars and historians are gnawing their fingernails off observing the Trump Administration chip away at the safeguards the founders of our great land worked so hard to put into place for us. Our forefather's "barriers" will only protect us as long as decent people stick together against any would-be autocrats. Instead, many of our current day legislators, along with foreign rulers and special interest groups that Trump has granted unprecedented access, have been sheltering and defending the wannabe dictator we have in power now.

Our forefathers likely didn't anticipate the influence that money and special interest groups would hold over our leaders. They also might not have envisaged that otherwise decent lawmakers would put their own jobs ahead of their country's welfare and have the audacity to protect any aspiring dictators. But perhaps they did consider the *risks* that such situations *might* occur. That could explain why they toiled so extra hard to create what they thought would be impenetrable checks and balances.

But never in their wildest nightmares could our forefathers have divined that specific interest groups would one day own television stations that could seize authority over the American people while they relaxed in their own living rooms. Nor could they have imagined that these self-serving manipulators of minds and messages would become direct advisers to the President, prompting *him* through the television set and daily phone conversations. Or that representatives of these groups could conceivably be granted offices *inside* the White House!

And our forefathers certainly could not have foreseen the Internet, or how it would provide foreign governments direct influence over American voters.

King Trump's perfect storm has landed!

Our main line of defense against this hijacking of our democracy comprises numerous individuals who are either taking or expecting favors themselves, or who are too terrified of losing their jobs (or who knows what else) to resist. It's merely a matter of time before all of Trump's dictatorial dreams become reality!

In the meantime, while Trump slides his fat ass further and deeper backward onto the king's throne, he does everything he *can* to hold off his distracters -- notably representatives of the press. But how much simpler it would be for him to retain his kingdom if he could just throw every last one of those naysayers in prison! Or maybe it would be better still if he could make them all just vanish?

Whew! Wouldn't *that* be something?

And we know Trump thinks that way. He's told us so himself.

While struggling to backpedal on a statement of his that suggested endorsement of the Chinese government's 1989 massacre of protestors in Tiananmen Square, Trump added this: "I said that is a strong, powerful government that put it down with strength. And then they kept down the *riot.*"

Trump has provided us with countless statements indicative of his reverence for tyrants. Surely Trump admires how effectively Kim Jong Un silences the opposition. No wonder Trump swears he "fell in love" with the barbarian.

Though Trump doesn't put in very many hours toiling on presidential matters, he does have to perform quite a bit of juggling to establish and sustain that throne of his. To start with (unlike the typical dictators that Trump envies) he had to get elected into the position in the first place.

Countless powerful forces and special interest groups (even at least one foreign government) helped Trump get elected. All these groups continue to pull strings for Trump in exchange for access and favors. These *elements* of our society realize that Trump is an open book, through which they've finally found *their* opening. They've observed how desperately Trump craves being king, and all they need do is flatter him and help maintain the child on his toy throne in exchange for the keys to the kingdom.

Trump's royal fantasies mean more to him than the welfare of the citizens he vowed to protect. The man who once purchased a life-size portrait of himself with his foundation's money, and the man who plastered phony images of Time magazine with himself on the cover at his various businesses, *must* be the king. At all costs. The question is -- does it matter even the slightest to him that in *this* country, in *his* kingdom, he can never be more than a puppet king?

Trump must continually appease the groups who helped plop his ass on that throne; he needs them to shield him from the majority of us who would love nothing more than to topple the tyrant. Trump knows as long as he maintains the support of the following groups, his kingdom is assured:

- *Religious Right*
- *Big Business*
- *Neo-Nazis*
- *Right Wing Commentators / News Media*
- *Working-Class Americans / His Base*
- *Russia / Putin*
- *Certain Republican Lawmakers*

If you observe Trump, you'll recognize that everything, absolutely EVERYTHING he says and does supports one of his objectives:

- **Making Money**
- **Being King**

We may never appreciate the winding backchannels and alleys our shadowy, shifty, shameless Svengali has to sleaze through to ensure a steady stream of precious cash. But yet, he's totally transparent when it comes to defending his monarchy. We can watch him in action right before our eyes. If you just tune in and observe, you'll notice that every word that passes his lips showcases the king -- placating the groups that, in one way or another, protect his throne. Whether he's granting access or favors to the various interest groups, or defending Neo-Nazi's, or favoring sworn enemies of the United States, he maintains his kingdom by kissing *someone's ass.*

All other times (when he's not watching himself on TV and stuffing his face with cheese burgers) you can find him gyrating on his platform, performing for his base.

Telling them what they want to hear . . .

Making them believe . . .

Brainwashing . . .

Vote Republican . . .
Vote for me . . .
You need me . . .
What would you ever do without me?

You are getting very sleepy . . .
When I count to three . . .

Whether or not we admit it, we all *know* in our hearts that Trump *is* The Shameless Svengali. The question we should be asking is: How much longer are we going to tolerate this self-seeking shyster, lolling around on his fat ass in The People's House (*Our House*) selling us off to the highest bidder, and continuing to profess that he's King over us all?

THE AUTHOR

I'm not a Democrat and no -- I didn't vote for Hillary, as many people who read this publication might assume. I'm not an Independent nor am I a Republican -- though last I checked I was still registered as one.

In the past I'd always voted across party lines -- for the candidate I felt best qualified. One election day that even meant writing in my mom.

Though I've probably voted primarily Republican throughout my life, I don't see myself voting that way again any time soon -- no matter how accomplished the candidate. Radical, biased *elements* have hijacked the Republican party, and far too many of its representatives have morphed into facilitators of the corrupt miscreants at the helm.

So . . . does that mean I'm a liberal or a Democrat now?

No . . . not really. And I certainly don't want to abolish ICE or anything like that.

What I *am* is fed up with the flagrant lies our leaders pass off to the American people as fact, in order to serve their own interests.

And no politician has ever been guiltier of that than Trump!

Trump's defenders would no doubt counter that all politicians lie.

I won't dispute that. In fact, I agree. Most politicians *do* lie, or at least stretch the facts. But I haven't always automatically considered that nefarious. We can't always be exactly certain why politicians lie. They could feel compelled to spout untruths to topple a corrupt candidate. Maybe they believe they must slant a few facts about legislation that might ultimately prove beneficial to us. Their lies and evasions really *could* be intended to protect us -- perhaps from the threats of other countries, or from learning things we'd definitely sleep much better at night never knowing.

Sadly, I haven't observed the slightest indication of altruistic motives behind any of Trump's blatant lies. Though the rationale of our leaders often remains shrouded in ambiguity, Trump's motivations are disturbingly clear.

His lies are ALL about him.

And those two damn lifetime goals of his.

1. **Be Rich**
2. **Be King**

Some people might still be thinking, what about what Hillary has done, or what about Obama, or what about so-and-so?

I urge anyone with knowledge of fraudulent, self-serving manipulation by any politician to inform the public.

Sooner rather than later.

Please, write your own books!

I'd love to read them.

This is *my* book.

It's about Trump.

The man who has spouted far more provable, self-serving lies to the American people than any private citizen, politician or president.

EVER!

I provided this brief background of my political persuasion (or lack thereof) so that readers wouldn't automatically infer that I had it in for Trump because of any conscious (or subconscious) ideologies. Though I am unapologetically repulsed by the man, Trump and Trump alone bears responsibility for the alienation.

Disclaimer: I don't claim to know Trump personally, thus I admit I can't present as "fact" what is in Trump's mind. (Nor could I even if I did know the man.)

When I mention things like "Trump thinks this, or knows this, or needs this, or doesn't like this, or he did this or that for one reason or another . . ." that is all based on reported information and personal observations of the Svengali in action!

The above disclaimer also applies to any motivations that might be "assigned" to anyone else mentioned throughout this book. All such indications should be construed as pure speculation on my part; I don't proclaim to know with certainty the *true* motivations of anyone.

But do contemplate the following . . .

Keen observations of a man's character are often more reliable indicators of the facts than any version of truth a Svengali might try to peddle.

"Character may almost be called the most effective means of persuasion."
-- **Aristotle**
"You could know a man not by what his friends said about him, but by how he treated his servants."
-- **Cassandra Clare, Clockwork Angel**

Contents

JUST BECAUSE

1. Are you Q?

If you live primarily in a fact-based world, hold on to your hats. Some Trump supporters believe in a clandestine "government insider", known to them by the moniker "Q". That "name" is based on this person's alleged high-level government security clearance. Q's followers call themselves "anons", thus generating the Q-anon movement. Q -- aka Q Clearance Patriot -- communicates with supporters via the Internet. This mysterious entity has convinced the true believers that our country has been in the grip of criminal presidents and other assorted evil politicians! Whew! Scary, right?

But never fear! Q to the rescue! Q is not only exceptionally smart and intuitive, Q is also extremely well-informed about governmental affairs -- thanks to that top-level security clearance! And this shadowy clearance holder has a plan to save our country from these evil, political scoundrels. Known by the anons as "The Storm" this transformational rescue always seems to be just around the bend. It's always . . . *coming*. Any day now! Wait for it. It's coming, they swear . . .

Amazingly, this rescue -- *that is always just around the corner* -- involves none other than -- *drumroll please* -- Donald J. Trump! Trump supposedly has allies in the military (a few of the good guys) who convinced *The Donald* to run for president. And now that Trump has indeed become the Master of the Universe, all of them are able to arrest the evildoers, ship them off to Guantanamo Bay, lock them up and throw away the key!

Lock them up! Lock them up!

Let us never forget -- these evil politicians (which naturally include Hillary and Obama) are the *real* colluders with Russia. We shouldn't blame Trump. Our man Trump is here to save us from the wicked ones -- who also happen to rape and murder children. If you're thinking no one could possibly believe all this crap -- think again! Remember *PizzaGate*?

One of the beliefs is that Trump could never have been involved with Russia himself, but the exceedingly clever Trump knew *all* about these criminal politicians from way waaayyyy back. That's our guy! He knows just about everything! Thank heavens he won the election and came up with this ingenious plan of his. All along he's been *pretending* to like Russia -- this way he could trigger an internal probe -- *think Mueller investigation* -- which would expose the truth about the *real* evil villains!

Smart! Right?

Got to hand it to whoever this Q person is! Getting out such urgent, classified info to the followers, and convincing them that all of it is real, took a ton of effort and guts!

Q keeps telling followers to wait for the storm, for the big purge.

Any day now . . . Wait for it . . .

But many of Trump's most susceptible followers want nothing more (albeit subconsciously) than to *keep* waiting. Trump swore he would lock Hillary up! He promised them. Again. And again. Hadn't he endlessly chanted the *lock her up* mantra with his base while they raised their arms and pledged to vote for him? Heck, he's still out there chanting this at his rallies. But has he delivered?

Nah!

Trump talks a good talk about how he's doing stuff he promised he would, but seldom does he *deliver*.

But this anticipation, this waiting for the swamp-sweeping storm gave hope to Trump's followers. Maybe their great leader, their idol, the magnificent drainer of all swamps, *did* have a plan to destroy the deep state and lock Hillary up. It *had* to be true!

There is nothing more crushing to the human psyche than to surrender oneself, to gift so much of one's personal energy into believing someone -- only to discover they've been lying to you or misleading you all along! Especially after you might have taken that *one* last chance on believing in someone after so many others have disappointed you. Q offered Trump's believers a chance to postpone the inevitable. To let them keep on believing in their man. Q ensured the followers that Trump was still out there, *secretly* draining that swamp; doing exactly what he had repeatedly promised them.

A smattering of celebrities -- *pretty much the usual suspects* -- signed on to this grand conspiracy theory. Alex Jones claimed he'd made personal contact with Q! Sean Hannity -- *of course, Sean Hannity* -- Trump's late-night phone buddy -- shared several Q-related tweets. Roseanne Barr soon insinuated herself into the clan. Barr tweeted to her followers: "we r the army of truth. wwg1wga" (which translates to, Where We Go One, We Go All). When anyone asks the Anons if they have proof of Q's existence, the set mantra response seems to be to ask the questioner if he has proof that Q *doesn't* exist!

Despite credible proof of *anything*, most of Q's followers are certain their leader is someone within the Trump organization -- maybe even Trump himself. After all, Trump is often heard stating that Hillary is the one who colluded with Russia. And when Trump speaks, he *does* often make a "Q" shaped *signal* with his fingers.

Q has been rather quiet lately. Could it be that Q has posted his last message? NBC may have unmasked "Q" as a group of three conspiracy theorists out to make money from all the Q merchandise. You heard right! Even though this is a clandestine society, anyone can purchase all of the movement's official gear on Amazon -- proving once and for all that Amazon does indeed have *everything*!

Makes you wonder -- what's next? For Q? For Q's followers? If Q sinks into total oblivion that will create a deep void . . . And nature so abhors a vacuum.

Makes you also wonder -- this movement helped perpetuate Trump's lies and kept his fans enchanted so he could keep playing King. The phenomenon also generated a heck of a lot of moola! Exactly the two results that Trump continually strives toward. Hmmmmm . . . Let's re-watch some of Trump's videos -- how *exactly* does he hold his fingers?

2. Did Rex Tillerson eat the salad?

While Trump and Tillerson were dining in a private room in China's Great Hall of the People, Trump worried that not eating the salad would insult their Chinese hosts. Gazing at Tillerson's plate of wilted Caesar salad, Trump reportedly commanded his top diplomat, "Rex, eat the salad."

3. Did Kim Jong Un ever get his CD?

It's reported that during Trump's historical Summit with Kim Jong Un (meant to promote denuclearization of the Korean peninsula) Trump felt it necessary to discuss the song *Rocket Man*, by Elton John, with the leader of North

Korea. (*Trump must have assumed that he had an inside, running gag with the Supreme Leader. Get it? Rocket Man?*)

For Secretary of State Pompeo's follow-up visit to North Korea, Trump gave Pompeo a *personally signed* (by Trump, not Elton John) CD containing the song to present to Kim Jong Un. Stories conflict as to whether Pompeo ever presented that special gift. It's said the North Korean leader did not meet with our Secretary of State on this visit and Pompeo had to return to the U.S. without making this momentous presentation.

WOULD YOU BUY A USED CAR FROM THIS MAN?

4. *Have you worked it all out yet, having Mexico pay for the wall?*

Even Trump's most fervent supporters realize by now that this was always BS! Some followers though are buying into the revised version of the promise -- that there are other ways Trump can make Mexico pay for the wall. Used car salesmen are searching far and wide for these people about now.

5. *Are you going ahead with the wall?*

Trump seized on a campaign promise to build the wall on the Mexican border, but only because it resonated well with his followers. He, and some of his Republican cronies seeking re-election, still see value in repeating the rallying cry -- in making followers continue to chant: "Build the Wall. Build the Wall." Trump pounced upon an existing fear of immigrants (within some American's hearts) and went with it. Never being satisfied with just scaring people a smidgeon, Trump drove people's fears to dizzying heights. "When Mexico sends its people, they're not sending their best," he proclaimed. "They're sending people that have lots of problems -- they're bringing drugs. They're bringing crime. They're rapists. And some, I assume, are good people."

Most of them *are* good people. Despite a few bad apples, immigrants have historically been more law-abiding than naturalized American citizens. But lots of people fell for Trump's hate speeches. Many still do.

Trump *has* taken numerous actions against immigrants that he thought would please his fearful followers as well as his most ardent financial backers and hate-filled advisers. He's had infants ripped from their mother's arms and left alone on cold concrete floors. He's had families separated without ever planning to reunite them. He's sent the military to the border, at an unbelievable expense to the taxpayers, and he's given the military the okay to shoot immigrants on sight if seemingly provoked. But with all that, is Trump going ahead with building the wall? It's one of his paramount campaign promises -- plus he's still encouraging his minions to chant about it. He keeps insisting it is being built.

It's got to be happening. Right?

Trump has proven skillful at convincing his followers he is delivering on his promises. One of the first things Trump did when taking office was issue an executive order to build the wall. He's had contractors build samples of walls (at great expense to the taxpayers) and has made sure we've all seen these samples numerous times. The White House bragged about the time when Pence paid a visit to the border, and Customs and Border Protection (CBP) officials briefed Pence on the wall's construction.

6. So . . . that must mean -- it's really gonna happen. Right?

Definitely not the way Trump promoted it.

He can sign as many executive orders as he damn well pleases, but (short of declaring a National Emergency or robbing from previously appropriated funds) unless he can get Congress to approve the funds, no one will ever build that wall. Besides, the wall (as Trump described it) is infeasible across many parts of the terrain in question.

It looks as if those eight hideous prototypes they constructed, for Trump to choose from for his "big, beautiful wall", were just exercises in futility. The Department of Homeland Security footed the bill for up to $4 million for that "exercise." And the Administration has so far stuck the taxpayers of San Diego with over $2 million to protect those prototypes. The Trump administration prefers to make us believe the personnel surrounding these senseless sections of wall are there protecting *people*, from possible protests.

Really? Tell us another one.

7. But we saw Vice President Pence -- standing there while they were building your wall. It's under construction -- just like you keep telling us. Right?

Pence *did* visit the wall. And CBP officials did brief him on the wall's construction. All that is true. But the White House led you to believe Pence was standing guard over *Trump's* wall. They made sure you could see that construction was going on, and it was. But all that construction was just *repair* work being done on an *existing* portion of the "wall," which is really more like a fence. Since Trump has been in office, Congress did finalize the funding for those repairs. But this had been in the works under the Obama Administration. This "construction" that Trump deemed to be the building of *his* wall, would have taken place *no matter who* was president.

8. But -- can't you make congress fund this wall?

Extremely unlikely! If the existing fence/wall needs additional repairs, then we'll likely see more action. Additional *sections* of wall may be built also, as deemed necessary. There are mixed reports, some stating that *small sections* of a Trump sponsored wall *are* in progress, but the Shameless Svengali will no doubt lie to us again and try to make us believe that *any and all* construction that you see is *his* wall.

It's even possible that Congress might approve additional funds for a *representational* section of wall just to appease Trump -- like when those bogus prototypes were built to pacify the whining baby. But they won't be building Trump's entire promised wall, as conceived and promised by Trump, no matter how hard The Shameless Svengali tries to convince us otherwise.

You might even hear Republicans occasionally mention their support for the wall. They must appease Trump so he can continue to brainwash his base. But will they build the damn thing? Don't fool yourself for one minute believing that members of Congress, *especially* Republicans, are eager to approve over **twenty-five billion** dollars on something most of them see as a wasteful indulgence. Except perhaps for Trump's Republican buddies on the far right – and the right-wing commentators who pull Trump's strings.

9. Do you still stand by your attacks on Obama when you claimed in at least twenty-seven tweets that he played far too much golf?

After tweeting excessively about how much golf Obama played while he was president, Trump is on track to play at least twice as much golf as President Obama ever did while in office. Trump's administration has claimed the president conducts high-level meetings on the golf course. Well, there was *one* time Trump golfed with a foreign official. And an occasional meeting may have taken place on Trump's golf course in which he bribed or threatened to blackmail a fellow Republican or two into seeing things his way. Other than that, Trump golfs with -- well, Trump prefers to keep that a secret -- though we know that many of his partners have been celebrity athletes and successful businessmen.

Whenever our president conducts high-level governmental meetings, (like the ones Trump claims to hold on the golf course) it's a requirement that the American people have a record of what transpired at these meetings. When a reporter pressed Trump's former White House spokesperson about when Americans would learn the results of these high-level, productive golf meetings, Sean Spicer retorted, "The president is entitled to a bit of privacy at some point."

Many of Trump's supporters will recall Trump's pledges to them: "I'm going to be working for *you*. I'm not going to have time to go play golf." And there was this: "If I win, I may never see my property -- I may never see these places again. But because I'm going to be working for *you*, I'm not going to have time to go golfing, believe me. Believe me. Believe me, folks."

And Trump's "folks" did believe him. Despite conclusive evidence to the contrary, many of Trump's followers still do.

WAS THERE ANY LIE TOO EXTREME, EVEN FOR THE SHAMELESS SVENGALI, BEFORE THE MIDTERM ELECTIONS?

In the one month leading up to the midterm elections, Trump made 815 documented false claims. We will question but a tiny percentage of them.

10. You told the American people it is the Democrat's fault that the caravan is coming? How so?

According to the border patrol, immigrant crossings have increased under Trump's watch. In fact, border crossings were the highest ever in September 2018, under a Republican President, a Republican Congress, and a Republican Senate. Yes, immigration issues have been plaguing our country for a long time. But Trump was the one who claimed to be our savior, the leader who would fix all those *annoying* issues. What happened? Under his leadership, it's gotten much worse.

So, what tactic does this "great" leader fall back on when he screws up? That's an easy one! He blames someone else. The Democrats are an easy target since he's painted them so black already. Trump insisted that *they* were behind the caravan! And although Shameless Svengali had zero proof to back his accusations, even that didn't stop him from spouting the lie. He even took it further, touting that this caravan was "good" for the Republicans, which only made the notion that the Democrats might be sponsoring the caravan even more ludicrous to clear-thinking people.

Trump even insisted that the caravan "invasion" wouldn't be happening if Democrats would only change the laws! And just how did Trump, even in his wildest, distorted imagination, ever fantasize that they could do that? In what universe would a Republican President, House, and Senate, who had shot down anything of real essence that the Democrats had proposed, sit back and let Democrats remake our country's immigration laws?

Trump and his far right Republican cronies were in a unique position to push through legislation. Shouldn't Trump have been working on something more productive? Like trying to work on actual solutions for some of these issues?

Nah!

Not our man Trump.

That would require concentration and reading -- Trump doesn't like to read -- unless the material is all about him.

He doesn't like complicated legislation and knows little about how that stuff works.

He doesn't even like burdening his brain with the daily presidential briefings, so let's not fantasize for even an instant about cluttering up this man's mind with intricate stuff he wouldn't understand.

But our deified leader has never been one to allow a small deficit like limited brain power stop him! Oh no! Not Trump! This man has rolled up his sleeves and showed the entire world *exactly* what he's made of! Let's see -- what are some of the steps he's taken so far to resolve our immigration issues?

Well -- he's ranted and raved about how it's all the Democrats' fault, even though they had no control over changing any laws. He's torn families apart -- and kept many of them apart -- without even having a plan to reunite them. He's wasted millions of dollars of our money in having phony prototypes built so his followers would think he was doing something and actually building his wall. He's thrown our military into the middle of the political arena, at another great cost to taxpayers and a risk to our security since our beloved military is sorely needed elsewhere. He has stated that he has given our guards at the border permission to shoot to kill if any immigrant should do so much as throw a rock, or who knows what else. He's had children locked up in cages. He's had suckling infants torn from their mother's breasts and left alone to cry their unseen tears on cold, concrete floors.

He's created complete havoc and legal issues with his Muslim travel ban, which did not include the countries that have posed the biggest terroristic threats to our country.

He's raved about how the coming caravan is an "invasion." He's conceivably inspired a man to gun down Jewish worshipers in their synagogue. (The man who massacred those innocent worshipers had claimed he couldn't take it anymore -- referring to a group of Jewish leaders he felt were supporting the "invasion" of our country by that same caravan.) Trump has scared his followers half to death with all this hype about the invaders coming to our country. (Even though we've seen plenty of these caravans before, which are generally protest marches that start out with thousands of marchers and in the past have ended up with a few hundred people *legally* seeking asylum into our country.) He's lied about there being middle easterners in the caravan to scare people even more. In Trump's usual fashion he has made his "contributions" to solving our problems well known.

11. Were you really planning to protect us from the immigrants in the caravan by calling in the military to close the border?

Trump caught even the Pentagon officials off guard with this one. Even after Trump made this announcement, they stated that they had not received any directives from the White House. Army Lt. Col. Jamie Davis, a Pentagon spokesman, stated that the Department of Defense had not been tasked to provide additional support.

Besides, Trump either doesn't know or conveniently failed to mention -- Federal law prohibits American service members from performing civilian law enforcement duties on U.S. soil outside of a military installation. Unless Trump declares a national emergency and Congress grants a waiver, deploying active U.S. military troops for domestic law enforcement duties is illegal. The last time Trump threatened to bring out the military, he had to drag out the National Guard to save face. They are under the command of the State Governors. Trump's use of the Guard has been mostly ineffective. They cannot detain or arrest suspected undocumented immigrants. Most of them cannot even carry weapons. Some of them help with surveillance, most of them perform administrative work and help to fix trucks and perform similar miscellaneous chores.

But what about the thousands of troops Trump did send to the border? They'll be protecting us from the people in the caravan, won't they?

Nah!

Trump tried to twist the Pentagon's arm on this, but they resisted. It's illegal. No matter how many times Trump thumps his chest and tries to convince his followers he is protecting us from an "invasion" and that he is the only one who *can* protect us, these troops will only be allowed to act in support roles. By the way -- since when do invaders give a country they're about to invade a notice of their plans months ahead of time? And don't invaders usually carry weapons? And use a heartier-looking group of attackers? Does anyone actually believe real invaders telegraph their invasions and have them televised months in advance, then arrive weaponless, with families with cut up feet and exhausted women pushing babies in strollers?

Trump declared "I am bringing out the military for the National Emergency. They will be stopped!" *Really?* Not by any of these troops, they won't. And even though Trump has been hinting at giving the military the right to fire at these immigrants, that is against the rules of engagement. Our military would have to disobey Trump's illegal command. (They've already pushed back on this.) Just how many of our fine young men and women do we think signed up to be in the services in the first place to go to the border and possibly kill law-abiding families who are merely seeking a better life?

Despite how many times Trump refers to these immigrants as evil lawbreakers, under the United States immigration law, people arriving at the border have a right to seek asylum. Trump is the one who will be breaking the law if he denies them that right. Our Shameless Svengali was just spreading his usual hatred and fear. He really wanted the Republicans to win in the midterms, and his method to achieve that had been garnering votes by scaring people half to death! Trump threatened to bring in even more troops. Note the words he used. "Invasion" and "National Emergency." He was *really* hoping he could get away with convincing us that this legal and orderly march of innocent, unarmed families toward our country was a national emergency. He likely hoped to bend that law so he could use the troops for the purpose of doing what Trump has already hinted he wants them to do: *Shoot 'em up!*

12. Is it true that people in California were rioting because they didn't want Sanctuary Cities?

No. That's false, another figment of Trump's imagination. As with all social issues, people in California often disagree with one another, but at the time of Trump's claim, there hadn't been anything even remotely resembling a riot. Not one. Not even a "teeny-tiny" one.

13. Were you really planning to give Middle Class Americans a ten-percent tax cut before the midterm elections?

No way. Congress wasn't even in session when Trump made the promise. Trump did later have to backtrack a bit after too many people pointed out that tax cuts were impossible before the midterm elections. Shameless Svengali revamped his lie and declared he would put in a resolution and give the cuts right *after* the midterms.

But what was this all about? Leading up to the midterm elections, Trump obviously began working on what someone had told him (which should have been obvious) were his "perceived" weaknesses. His constant lying is clearly one of those sore spots, but most members of his base don't seem to give a damn about that. But they might have cared about that "big" tax cut that The Shameless Svengali had provided to our country. If anyone had taken the time to examine the specifics, he would realize that this cut mostly benefited Trump, and other very wealthy people. It was good for businesses (by far the best for the business structure that Trump always uses), but there wasn't all that much in it for the middle class. Some claim to have done okay; others speak of receiving an extra $1.25 a week in their paychecks. Many others will end up paying more -- especially in states that lean mostly democratic, *fancy that*! Even the few middle-classers who saw something decent in their finances from Trump's tax break have long since seen it eaten away by inflation and increased health insurance premiums.

Not seeing much of this gigantic tax break (the biggest in American history according to Trump -- another lie) is something that might have made more than a few of Trump's supporters sit up and wonder what the hell was going on. Especially since the alleged tax cut to the middle class is only temporary, while the rich get to bask in their windfalls for -- well for eternity if Trump and the special interest groups he caters to have anything to do with it. But Trump figured he had the answer. A way to appease his base. He would tell them (just ahead of the midterm elections) that there would be a ten-percent tax cut -- *just* for the middle class.

Representative Kevin Brady of Texas, the Republican Chairman of the House Ways and Means Committee, had suddenly, *supposedly* been working on this tax cut for months. Guess they supposed no one would notice it was odd that he couldn't provide any details of the plan he'd allegedly been slaving over for months. But Trump did twist the man's arm hard enough to make him issue this statement: "Republicans will continue to work with the White House and Treasury over the coming weeks to develop an additional ten-percent tax cut focused specifically on middle class families and workers, to be advanced as Republicans retain the House and Senate."

REALLY?? So the middle class could ONLY get their little piece of the American pie IF they voted straight down the Republican ticket?

But seriously now -- under any circumstances -- did anyone actually believe the middle class would be getting this tax cut? Even if Republicans did retain the House and Senate? Believe that one and maybe Trump himself will sell you a used car. Maybe one of those Rolls-Royces that Trump swore the Democrats would be giving away to immigrants to incentivize them to cross our borders. Generous people, those Democrats, *hey*?

And you know, even if Republicans lost the House or the Senate they would still have several months left where they *could* push through the promised tax cuts. Would they do it? As promised?

Nah!

The answer is clear. Most Republicans didn't even know a thing about this tax cut. Trump's supporters heard it FIRST!

Paul Ryan's office got flooded with calls asking if this middle-class tax cut was for real. They referred all those callers to the White House. Kevin Hassett, the chairman of the White House Council of Economic Advisers, also referred questions to the White House press office, adding that the person discussing this right now was the President, so we should get our information from him.

Neither could Treasury Secretary Steven Mnuchin offer any details of the plan that even lobbyists hadn't heard a thing about. What about tax analysts? What did they know about the plan? Nothing. Nada. Zero. And Steven M. Rosenthal of the Tax Policy Center? Surely, *he* had heard something? When asked about it, he responded, "No idea really."

Here's a sampling of how Trump attempted to explain the discrepancy:

A **Reporter** mentioned that Trump wanted lower tax cuts by November 1. The reporter asked how that was possible when Congress wasn't even in session.

Mr. Trump: No, we're going to be passing -- no, no. We're putting in a resolution sometime in the next week, or week and a half, two weeks.

Reporter asked where this resolution would be.

Mr. Trump: We're going to put in -- we're giving a middle-income tax reduction of about 10 percent. We're doing it now for middle-income people. This is not for business; this is for middle. That's on top of the tax decrease that we've already given them.

Reporter asked if Trump was signing an executive order for that.

Mr. Trump: No. No. No. I'm going through Congress.

Reporter reiterated that Congress wasn't in session.

Mr. Trump: We won't have time to do the vote. We'll do the vote later.

In response to worries about our country's ballooning federal budget deficit, Trump further clarified: "We're putting in a tax reduction of 10 percent, which I think will be a net neutral, because we're doing other things, which I don't have to explain now, but it will be pretty much a net neutral. But it will be great for the middle class. It's going to be a tax reduction of 10 percent for the middle class."

What Trump no doubt didn't feel he had to explain now (or likely ever) is how much he'd have to cut the federal budget to pay for those tax cuts. Like just how much food he'd have to rip out of the mouths of hungry children, or benefits he'd have to strip away from our grandparents or our future retired selves, etc. etc.

No matter how many phony resolutions Trump had the Republicans scramble to throw together to allow Trump to save face, remember one thing. Those resolutions were all "non-binding."

People really should ask themselves -- if Trump couldn't even convince the Senate to make the measly middle-class tax cuts permanent, how did he plan on convincing them to give the middle class an additional ten percent? *Permanently?*

14. Is it true that Democrats refused to support the opioid bill?

Many of us witnessed the pompous ceremony Trump presented while signing the opioid bill. He tooted his own horn and blasted the Democrats for their opposition. According to Trump, he and his Republican cronies had a real tough time pushing this bill through, which is crucial to help the American people combat an ever-burgeoning crisis. But luckily for us, the Republicans (under Trump's benevolent guidance, of course) pressed on and got the bill passed, even with, "very little Democrat support."

Wow! This once again "proves" just how amazing Trump can be. And to think, this sounds exactly like the type of bill that the Democrats would have liked to get behind -- but yet -- according to Trump, he had "very little Democrat support."

Could that be true? Do we have only Trump and the Republicans to thank for finally addressing this epic crisis?

Let's look at how the Senators voted to get our true answer. In a rare Senate vote, the results were practically unanimous, amongst both Republicans *and Democrats.* You would think Trump might have used this legislation as an example of how both sides could come together and do something good for our country. Trump could have figured out a way, *somehow,* to make himself look good in that assessment. He could have declared something about how only he could make the far-left and the far-right come together! Something silly like that. But, oh no, not Trump. That wouldn't have been good enough for Trump. Better to keep on blatantly lying. Keep on dividing us. Use this opportunity to make his base despise the Democrats even more.

Now, getting back to the truth.

There was ONE Senator who opposed this bill. Could that be the democratic opposition the Shameless Svengali had ranted about? Does that mean that there could be a smidgen -- no matter how far-fetched -- no matter how tiny -- of truth to Trump's statement?

Nah!

The one naysayer, the only Senator who offered any "resistance" was Mike Lee, of Utah.

A *Republican.*

15. You keep saying you don't want to lose your 114-billion-dollar arms deal with Saudi Arabia. Especially since you are informing us that through this deal you can create OVER a million jobs for us! Are those figures accurate?

Nope. Not even close!

Little, if *any,* of the junk that comes out of the Shameless Svengali's mouth, when he boasts about his personal accomplishments, is correct. Trump is hailing this as *his* bill, even calling it his *signature achievement*! Not so fast -- Trump had nothing to do with originating this deal. It had been in place since the Obama Administration.

And it's not even really a deal. It's mostly just a bunch of letters of intent or interest or offers for potential future sales.

And those statistics that Trump is citing -- shame, shame, *shame.* They are even more *Trumpian* than his usual BS! When Trump talks about how this deal will mean over a million jobs for Americans, one must wonder if this is the same deal he had started out declaring *could possibly* provide 40,000 jobs?

Yep. Same one.

Sounding like a crazed bidder who *must* win an item at auction, Trump kept raising that estimate. (The job predictions seemed to spike the most just as the world's disgust of Saudi Arabia peeked, following the vicious murder and dismemberment of an innocent reporter. Also, as the midterm elections zeroed in, the numbers shot up even further.)

Right away the number of jobs "Trump's" deal with Saudi Arabia would mean for Americans shot up from 40,000 to 45,000. All right -- that's okay; there's always room for a *little* leeway. But the increments in which those numbers kept increasing came faster than ever. Trump's job prediction totals quickly jumped to 500,000 then to 600,000, then to a million, then to *over a million* jobs!

Why not two million?

Come now, we've come this far.

What's wrong with a billion?

Speaking of billions, the deal itself brought in, or was supposed to bring in, 114 billion dollars to our country! Pretty decent, right?

Well, it *would* be, but according to a 2017 draft list of deals in the arms package, *they defined 95 billion dollars of this deal* as memorandums of intent/non-binding commitments. When asked for a clarification on this, The White House did not immediately respond.

Thus far the so-called 114-BILLION-dollar bill has provided us with 14.5 billion in purchases.

Something to brag about, yes, but the actual figures are so far from what IS being bragged about.

And what about all those jobs Trump promised? Even if not a million, certainly *many* jobs will be created?

Not exactly! Jim Corridore, Director of Industrials Research, of the research and investment firm CFRA Research, stated, "It's not going to create or take away a single job, I don't think. There are other homes for these products should these deals fall through."

Other industry experts claim the same. The big "Trump deal" might not even create one single job.

Maybe Trump should learn to count backward? OVER one million jobs -- one million jobs -- six-hundred thousand -- five-hundred thousand -- forty-five thousand -- forty thousand -- **ZERO jobs**!

16. You act as if people seeking asylum in this country is something new when it's as old as our country itself. You like to ramble about how you're going to protect us from the supposedly bad people in the caravan. But, tell us, do you plan on protecting us when we face real terrorism?

Nah!

America *has* faced real terrorism since Trump took office. Homegrown terrorism in the form of mailed, potentially explosive pipe bombs. Only people who had somehow opposed Trump received these bombs. After the bomber's arrest, authorities discovered that numerous other people, most of whom Trump had publicly criticized, were on the list to receive similar bombs. It became apparent to many that Trump's harsh criticism of those who didn't bow down and support him had inspired this assailant to commit these dangerous deeds.

How did Trump respond to these domestic terroristic threats?

Pretty much how we'd predict. With the lack of enthusiasm we expect when he's being coerced into doing something, Trump read a teleprompter statement. He showed zero empathy for the recipients of the potentially life-threatening bombs while mumbling off some statement about how we must all unite in these troubled times. He did this after coming under severe criticism for his harsh rhetoric of the press and others, particularly since they were the ones receiving these bombs. But after quickly reading his prepared statement, Trump put that press conference behind him. Then he responded in the way he'd been dying to.

Don't tell me you don't know what our predictable Shameless Svengali did next?

He came out swinging! In true Trump fashion he blamed others for the terrorist attacks upon innocent Americans -- the attacks he himself had more than likely inspired. While bombs (that could have killed *anybody)* were still coursing through America's mail system, Trump declared that this was all the media's fault!

He claimed many of the people who had received the bombs were guilty of inspiring those bombs to land in their *own* mailboxes!

Trump hoped this diversion would help Republicans snatch a few more votes come Election Day! Trump so loves to rally his base against one of its favorite bogeymen: the "fake news" media. He wrote on Twitter: "A very big part of the Anger we see today in our society is caused by the purposely false and inaccurate reporting of the Mainstream Media that I refer to as Fake News. It has gotten so bad and hateful that it is beyond description. Mainstream Media must clean up its act, FAST!"

Besides *this* blatant example of not caring for the American people, after a journalist who resided in the United States had been horrifically murdered and dismembered, Trump was right back out there rallying the crowds -- condoning violence against the press. He even acted out, with vigorous enthusiasm and great appreciation, an incident where a Republican politician had body-slammed a reporter.

Words such as these can only encourage diehard Trump supporters to commit even more dastardly deeds. Trump has the power to tone down the rhetoric from that big influential soapbox of his. He could help to decrease the chances of similar future violence. But does he want to use the power of his words to help protect American citizens from further violence?

Nah!

The Shameless Svengali prefers to scare his base half to death while providing them with a common enemy to despise. If they remain focused on hating this shared enemy, they can never see the real monster, the one hiding in plain sight, just behind Trump's mask.

Trump loves to believe he's convinced everyone that he's unique. That all the *rallying up the base* nonsense is *his* invention. But that too is just another of his infinite deceptions. He's just following an old, overused playbook that's been around since the beginning of time. All the world's most evil dictators have used these same tactics. What's really scary is -- while these methods have worked in the past, and we're all aware that history repeats itself, we're still allowing history *to* repeat itself. People are still buying into these ancient playbooks. And as long as The Shameless Svengali can keep enough of them hypnotized, Trump (or one of his descendants) will continue to play the king -- or maybe they'll alter our fine country so much to their liking that one of them will actually *be King*!

17. Is it true you want to bring drug prices down to help Americans?

Too little. Too late. Trump *had* promised us during his campaign he would *take on* the pharmaceutical industry and be our big brave hero; he would force drug companies to lower their prices for all of us. But, in true Trump fashion, after his campaign victory, he emerged from a meeting with those same pharmaceutical lobbyists and executives he was going to "take on." No sooner did the door hit Trump in the ass that he promised tax cuts and deregulation FOR the drug companies. Even if Trump's latest proposal to lower drug prices were to take effect, it would take *years* to phase in the price adjustments. Besides, the proposal would likely face fierce resistance from drug makers. From those same people that had sent Trump scrambling to do *their* bidding the first time he'd met them. Health care providers and even some Republicans would also likely offer resistance.

And you want to know the *real* irony of Trump's latest deception? His administration claimed they could carry out this proposal (lowering our drug prices) by using the Center for Medicare and Medicaid Innovation, which had been created as part of the *Affordable Care Act.* Are they for real? *The Affordable Care Act?* The same program that Trump has done everything in his power to *abolish?* The same program that Senator John McCain had voted against abolishing -- the vote that Trump has been mocking McCain about ever since? Even long after the man has been dead and buried?

Yep, the same one.

And as we "speak" Trump is chipping away at that program, doing everything he can to make it collapse. Yes, that SAME program would be the one he would have to use to fulfill his promise of lowering our drug prices.

18. Do you Really Want to Protect Those of us that have Pre-existing conditions?

Absolutely not. Another false pre-election promise. Trump and the Republicans have done everything in their power to repeal the Affordable Care Act, which contains that provision, which most Americans now rely upon. Trump taunted Senator John McCain, even long after his death, for throwing a wrench into Trump's precious plans to do away with the Affordable Care Act. The Shameless Svengali's plan was to screw Americans out of their health insurance and insurance protections and make more money for big business -- *you know the drill by now* -- so that those big businesses would keep on supporting Trump as the king.

Besides, the Republicans had demonized Obamacare for so long, they'd brainwashed countless Americans into believing the plan was evil. Trump saw this as an opportunity to make his base think that as he abolished the plan, he was doing something *for* them.

But let's not forget, it *is* the Affordable Care Act, AKA Obamacare, that guarantees us protection from those who would deny us reasonably-priced health insurance based on pre-existing conditions.

Every *single* Republican voted against The Affordable Care Act and the benefits it would bring to the American people.

In fact, The Trump Administration introduced a sweeping new policy to allow states to sidestep Obamacare's requirement to cover pre-existing conditions.

Fewer Regulations = Bad for Americans = Good for big business = More money for the rich!

So, as Trump works toward getting rid of protections for Americans, he satisfies big business. He wipes their asses, they wipe -- well, you get the picture. But this creates another issue for Trump: Most Americans (including his followers) like the protections offered to them under The Affordable Care Act! (Even though they've been brainwashed into despising Obamacare itself, many of them are *on* Obamacare and don't even realize it, *go figure.*) Remember, if Trump wants to keep on being king, he must appease his followers as well. The poor, poor dear. *Such a delicate balancing act!*

But not for Trump. He took care of this "minor issue" using his go-to method. He spread a pack of lies. He swore at his rallies he would protect the people who had invested so much into protecting him. He tweeted: "Republicans will protect people with pre-existing conditions far better than the Dems!"

Once he finished deceiving the crowd, he no doubt wiped his palms together and washed his hands of the entire matter.

There.

Done!

There goes another line of old jalopies -- being driven right off Trump's used car lot!

19. ***Did you have anything to do with the scheme before the midterm elections where someone hired a woman to say Robert Mueller had sexually assaulted her? At least one reporter who'd been investigating that story received serious threats.***

Just wondering, since it has your fingerprints smeared all over it.

20. ***Why wouldn't you cancel your rally right after the pipe bomb mailings and Synagogue attack?***

Trump explained that he had thought about canceling a rally, right after Americans suffered a vicious week of domestic terrorism. Yes, Trump *considered* canceling until -- he "remembered" something. He recalled that in 2001, the stock market had re-opened the day after September 11. Therefore, if the stock market could be back in business the day after terrorists viscously slaughtered thousands of innocent people, why couldn't Trump run off to his rally right after a madman gunned down eleven Jewish congregants while they worshipped in their synagogue? And what did it really matter if explosive pipe bombs, sent to Trump's most vocal critics, were still making their way through our mail system?

If the stock market could reopen right after such a vicious terrorist attack, Trump should go to his rally!

Makes sense! *Right?*

Not to any logical minds.

Trump not only "remembered" that the stock market reopened on September 12, 2001, he also supplied precise details. According to Trump, a close friend of his was the one who accomplished this amazing deed. Trump couldn't resist bragging about his very resourceful buddy: "He said what they had to do to open it you wouldn't believe, we won't even talk to you about it. But he got that exchange open. We can't make these sick, demented, evil people important."

As usual, Trump left himself wide open for a reality check! After the horrific events of September 11, 2001, the New York Stock Exchange remained closed until the following week. It reopened on September 17, 2001.

21. Are you really going to be able to kick out those Americans -- people who were born here -- but had illegal immigrant parents?

No!

As with so many other of Trump's brainy ideas, he obviously figured this one sounded good to his supporters. And he'd do anything to sound good to them. But the law that governs this, the one that Trump claims to be able to change with a stroke of the pen, is written into the constitution. There isn't an executive order in the world capable of changing that. Don't believe it? Ask the attorney who did the legal work on immigration for the First Lady and who helped Melania's parents become U.S. citizens. He, along with countless other legal experts, have confirmed that Trump cannot change that law on a whim.

Trump would have you believe he can fight the law even if it is an official amendment to the Constitution. He would also have you believe current-day Democrats have something to do with the amendment that allows children of immigrants born in this country to automatically become citizens of the United States. The constitutional amendment, that Trump swears he will knock out with a stroke of his pen, was written in *1866*. Modern-day Democrats had a hand in *that*? Boy oh boy, that Chuck Schumer sure looks good for his age!

Trump also armed Mike Pence with a stack of false statements about how the Supreme Court had never taken up this amendment.

Wrong!

Trump would also have you believe since he "controls" the Supreme Court now, the justices are just in place, waiting to do his bidding. Fact is, he's put two men on the Supreme Court who follow the Constitution, *as it was written*. And the text of the constitutional amendment to which Trump is referring is exceedingly clear -- which is why it's been the law of the land for nearly two centuries.

22. Are you not beyond bashing anyone -- even leaders in your own party, if one of them tells the truth about your lies?

Regarding Trump stating that he planned to do away with the fourteenth amendment with the stroke of a pen, Paul Ryan (in agreement with most legal scholars) pointed out that Trump did not have the authority to strip the right of citizenship from individuals born in the United States to illegal immigrant parents.

Trump fired right back on Twitter: "Paul Ryan *should be focusing on holding the Majority* rather than giving his opinions on Birthright Citizenship, something he knows nothing about! Our new Republican Majority will work on this, Closing the Immigration Loopholes and Securing our Border!"

Leading up to the midterm elections, Ryan campaigned exhaustively in at least 12 states. He raised over $70 million for Republicans that were running for House re-election.

I dunno . . . the man does sound pretty focused . . .

As Trump must always have the final word, he proclaimed that the Supreme Court would settle the matter.

23. Really? The caravan is filled with terrorists who are all coming to destroy us?

Trump (and now Pence) have repeatedly insisted that the caravan is full of "Middle Easterners". Even though most Middle Easterners are peace-loving people, it's clear that this statement, repeated incessantly in a derogatory manner, implied that terrorists are invading our country. It's meant to divide and scare us. Divide and conquer us. In

Trump's mind, if he can convince his followers that only he can save them from these invading terrorists, they'd have to vote Republican. And guess what would happen then? Trump could keep on playing king, of course!

But we can't let all his Middle Easterner BS fool us. Not for one second. Trump is more pro Middle Easterner than most of us. Ever notice how Saudi Arabia and Egypt were not on his Muslim travel ban list? Why would *that* be? Especially since most of the September 11th terrorists were *from* Saudi Arabia and the leader of the terrorists, who piloted the first plane smack into the North Tower of the World Trade Center, was an Egyptian.

And yet, Trump is sending out the military, claiming they'll hold off the people in the caravan. The *families* who want little more than to have their chance to legitimately apply for asylum in this country, just like many of our ancestors did. As of the time of this writing, Trump wants to send about *five* members of the military for every *one* man, woman or child in the caravan. And that's in addition to all the Border Patrol agents and National Guard troops that are already there. Considering that history has shown us that as the caravan continues, the number of approaching people falls drastically, and if you add up the members of security already on our border, figure there would be *at least* six or seven of *us* to every one of *them*. Add in the fact that the members of our "resistance" will be well-rested and fortified while the people in the approaching caravan will be exhausted and starving, having just trekked thousands of miles through the roiling desert.

And the people from the countries that perpetrated September 11 are free to keep flying in and out of our country -- whenever they damn well please.

Oh wait, wait a minute. Wait just one minute now. Let's reconsider the only two goals that Trump has had in his life: Be King! Make Money! Well then, it all makes sense now. It's no secret he's made a ton of money off the Saudis. And he stands to make endless more big bucks off them by their visiting entourages staying at Trump hotels. Why on Earth would he give *them* any grief?

Better for the Shameless Svengali's bottomless pockets if he works Americans into a frenzy over the "fake news" and the "invaders" and molds our minds into believing that only the Republicans can protect us!

Yay! Vote Republican. Vote Republican. A win - win for all.

We all know more votes for Republicans means Trump gets to keep on playing the king. Scaring the pants off people has worked in the past to help Trump achieve that goal -- so all the pieces of the puzzle do fit neatly into place.

Except for one. The taxpayers are footing the bill for Trump's election stunt. This latest whim of his will cost Americans up to $110 million! Considering that the average cost of building a mile of road in the United States is $675,000, Trump could have used our money for more productive purposes than propping up his chest so he could thump on it some more. We should think about that the next time we're stuck in traffic on some crumbling road or forking over our hard-earned bucks to repair our pot-hole ravaged cars. Oh wait, don't some of us have an extra $1.25 in our weekly paychecks? That's got to help. *Right*?

Trump is sending more troops to the border than he is using to fight ISIS. Ouch!

And considering those troops can only perform limited duties, double Ouch!!

Trump even sent Pence out to back up his lies about terrorists in the caravan. Pence prefers to keep a low profile, and keep his lies somewhat in check, but not this time. After bumbling his way through a press conference with Trump, twisting statistics to back up Trump's false claims, Trump cut Pence right off while Pence was stuttering, attempting to do Trump's bidding. Despite tossing out a bunch of unrelated statistics about stopping terrorists, neither Trump nor Pence could offer any proof that terrorists were in the caravan. Even so, Trump kept repeating his cross-armed utterings about how he had *very good information* about his claims! When pressed he could not come up with even one source of this *very good information*. Even though an endless sea of reporters had been traveling WITH the caravan and had *all* reported that there were *not any* Middle Easterners in the caravan, Trump and Pence kept insisting there were. They tried their damnedest to keep us all petrified, just before the elections.

Eventually, one of Trump's "favorite" reporters, Jim Acosta of CNN, got Trump to admit that they did not have *any* proof that Middle Easterners were in the caravan. Unfortunately for Pence, he had already publicly shamed himself by uttering the ridiculous statement that: "It's inconceivable there are not people of Middle Eastern descent in the caravan." This seems eerily reminiscent of the Q followers who defend the existence of their beloved leader by stating that others don't have proof that Q *doesn't* exist. But these utterings by our *Vice President* are even more ludicrous than those of the Q followers. In this case, we DO have proof that Middle Easterners are NOT in the caravan.

While we're on the subject, why not ponder this? Don't terrorists like to keep a low profile? Would they *really* hook up with a caravan of people that are being filmed and projected on news stations across the globe? And why would Middle Eastern terrorists take such a roundabout route to do their dirty deeds? Why would they submit themselves to a two-thousand-mile trek across the dry, acrid desert in the stifling, excruciating heat while listening to babies whining and screaming all the way? Especially when voluptuous stewardesses could be serving them delicious and refreshing cocktails in the well-air-conditioned comfort of first class? After which they could lean back on their big, comfy airplane headrests -- and fly straight in to America.

24. Did you ever think of doing something constructive about our immigration issues?

If the approaching caravan comprises terrorists who will bring nothing but doom and gloom and danger to our country, one would think Trump might consider doing something that might actually curtail these invading armies. I mean, if we need to send out troops -- more than are fending off ISIS -- to *immediately* head off these "invaders" while they are still thousands of miles away, why not do something that would actually decrease their numbers? Many of the migrants are coming for asylum, claiming they are escaping violence in their own countries. But why are they coming *here*, specifically?

For the jobs, stupid!

Our economy *is* doing well. Jobs, jobs, jobs, as Trump loves to claim. And these "invaders" know if they can only make it here, their pick of a job will be waiting. Why doesn't Trump invest time into cracking down on the people who continually *hire* the illegal immigrants? If no one hired them in the first place, there'd be no incentive for them to "invade" our country to look for work.

But wait a minute -- Trump's rich buddies -- his donors wouldn't like that. After all, *they* are the ones who like to hire the people who will slave for them for practically nothing. And Trump himself has a documented history of taking advantage of the hard-working "invaders".

Trump's businesses have often hired illegal immigrants. The Trump organization has even been reported to have run a little *side business* of procuring phony identification papers and social security numbers for these "invaders" so Trump can take full advantage of them and slide some more money into his slippery pockets. Trump knows these "invaders" will be extremely grateful to him for "sponsoring" them in the United States, (even if the entire process is illegal). Trump counts on them to work extra hard for him, and for far less money than the average *legal* citizen would work.

Makes you wonder -- is that why Trump kidnapped all those immigrant children? Does he and his rich buddies have plans for these ill-fated children?

RANDOM EVENTS

25. Your attorney, Jay Sekulow, called for a "time out on this inquiry", referring to the Mueller investigation into Russian meddling. Is he for real? Did you sort of, kind of, suggest this ridiculous tactic?

There's always much speculation about *when* someone in Trump's administration (who has anything to do with the Mueller investigation) will be canned. There has been talk, on and off, that Rosenstein might be the next to go. As soon as that talk sounded serious, Sekulow announced that if that happened (Rosenstein leaving) a "time out" in the investigation would be in order. You mean like, Mueller should take a break? Or maybe he's hinting that Mueller should drop the whole thing all together? What would be the reasoning for this? People are *working* on this investigation. Should they all drop everything they're doing and take a *vacation*?

Imagine if your favorite baseball team had a managerial change. Should the players all go on vacation? Like -- maybe they should take a time-out from the World Series or something? How would ticket holders react to the whole team just vanishing because there were changes in the back office?

And yet, Sekulow insisted: "It clearly becomes necessary and appropriate . . . that there be a step back taken here, and a review."

Necessary? Really?

Appropriate? Give us a break!

Hasn't Trump and his team even considered how guilty these types of statements make them look?

26. Can you please tell us what marketing guru suggested the military term "search and destroy" be used as a Right-Wing battle cry?

During the Kavanaugh confirmation hearings, Republicans united in their rallying call using the military term "search and destroy" to characterize the tactics of the Democrats. Brett Kavanaugh even used it in his "rebuttal" speech. "This confirmation process has become a national disgrace," he said in his opening statement. "The Constitution gives the Senate an important role in the confirmation process, but you have replaced 'advice and consent' with 'search and destroy.'" Kavanaugh swore he'd written the statement *himself* the night before. What a coincidence then that so many other Republicans all started using "his" phrase right around the same time. The term which had previously been associated with military campaigns, computer virus software, movies about war, and rock bands, suddenly sprung up as the latest shaming "motto" for Republicans to use against Democrats. Hopefully, the American taxpayers didn't have to pay big bucks to whoever the marketing "genius" was that dreamed up that all-encompassing catch phrase.

27. Hey! When do you plan on giving Elizabeth Warren the million dollars you promised?

As is his penchant for giving nicknames, Trump has often attempted to belittle Elizabeth Warren by calling her Pocahontas. He's also claimed Warren lied when she stated she had some American Indian blood in her veins. In July he stated he would toss a DNA test on stage if he ever debated her adding, "I will give you a million dollars, paid for by Trump, to your favorite charity if you take the test and it shows you're an Indian. And we'll see what she does. I have a feeling she will say no."

Now that Senator Warren has taken the test, and it showed "strong evidence" of Native American ancestry, she requested that Trump: "Please send the check to the National Indigenous Women's Resource Center," a non-profit group that helps protect Native American women from violence.

Trump initially denied to reporters he ever issued the challenge: "Who cares? I didn't say that. You better read it again," he proclaimed. Some might question the circumstances that initiated the bet, or if Warren totally proved her claim. But recognizing that Trump, his mini-me son Don, Jr., and his spokespeople reacted in their usual childish, combative, nonsensical and bullish fashion to Warren's test results, most people think Trump should just bite the bullet and fork the money over. Whatever the circumstances, a bet is a promise. And although some could call into question specifics of the bet, in reality Trump lost. Didn't he?

Trump claims to be a self-made billionaire. He can afford it. Right? And it is a good cause. But wait a minute - - isn't Trump the guy who wouldn't even fork over the (chump change) $10,000 he'd pledged for the September 11th rescue workers? Yep, the same guy. The brave souls who risked and gave their lives on that fateful day were Trump's fellow New Yorkers. Trump was only a few blocks away when the towers crumbled, and still, Trump would not make good on his promise to those workers.

Chances are the indigenous women might as well kiss any hope of Trump's donation goodbye.

28. Do you think making fun of Elizabeth Warren helped Melania's "Be Best", Anti-Bullying Campaign?

Melania stood behind Trump as he mocked Elizabeth Warren over the DNA test. Though Melania initially had a big, broad smile on her face, it quickly turned into a cold, hard stare as Trump continued "Being Trump." Though he probably *was* "being best" . . . at least the best for him.

29. What was the real purpose of your lashing out at Stormy Daniels on Twitter? Do you think that helped Melania's "Be Best" campaign?

Trump won *one* of the battles in *one* of Stormy Daniels' legal cases against him. True, the case will go into appeals, but things looked good for Trump. The judge ordered Stormy to pay Trump's legal fees. The most presidential thing Trump could have done with this information would have been nothing. Zero. Zilch. Nada. Everyone would have *known* he'd won. He could have gloated to himself, then watched himself on the news -- *as he constantly does* -- and he might have even come across as *sort of presidential*. Or better yet, he could have busied himself doing things that a president should be doing. Doesn't he have one of the busiest jobs on Earth? Shutting his fat trap for once would have made his accusers look bad and him look good. But Trump couldn't leave it at that. Oh no! Not our boy. He felt compelled to gloat. In a big way!

Why he felt it necessary to comment on *this* case, when he's been involved in *nearly* FOUR **THOUSAND** lawsuits in his lifetime, (most of them much more complex) is unclear. One can only guess that since this case, (a minor blip within a lifetime of lawsuits) had been sensationalized, Trump felt an irresistible urge to dramatize it even further, with something that would take off on social media and get the American people battling against one another over him. His ego requires this. *Plus, his base enjoys this sort of banter.*

Trump sent a tweet threatening to go after Ms. Daniels and her "third-rate lawyer." He referred to Stormy as "Horse Face."

But the insults came to a screeching halt after Stormy shot back, referring to Trump as "Tiny."

30. What happened to that cheap gas you promised us?

Trump's Tweet from June 2018: "Just spoke to King Salman of Saudi Arabia and explained to him that, because of the turmoil and dysfunction in Iran and Venezuela, I am asking that Saudi Arabia increase oil production, maybe up to 2,000,000 barrels, to make up the difference... Prices to (sic) high! He has agreed!"

The state-run Saudi Press Agency ran a statement regarding that same call, which didn't quite line up with Trump's version: "During the call, the two leaders stressed the need to make efforts to maintain the stability of oil markets and the growth of the global economy." The Saudis went on to say that oil-producing countries would need "to compensate for any potential shortage of supplies."

Even the White House couldn't back Trump on his tweet; they released this wishy-washy statement: "King Salman affirmed that the Kingdom maintains a two-million barrel per day spare capacity, which it will prudently use if and when necessary to ensure market balance and stability, and in coordination with its producer partners, to respond to any eventuality."

Oil prices will *increase even more*, in large part, because of the Trump administration pushing allies to end all purchases of oil from Iran after the U.S. pulled out of the Iranian nuclear deal. Gas prices during the summer of 2018 were up 24% from the year before, the highest in four years. In Trump's usual fashion of blaming someone else for all the negative outcomes he has created, he continually lashed out at Saudi Arabia to release more oil. Experts say Saudi Arabia and Russia combined are incapable of replacing Iran's production after sanctions kick in, and Russia will expect hefty price hikes for any added production.

Trump's constant pressure also caused Saudi Arabia to release oil too soon, before the Iranian sanctions kicked in, causing an overproduction. (That's Trump's way of making himself look good, he was likely hoping that would make gas prices go down!) Despite the overproduction, Trump kept harassing the Saudis to produce more. Finally, the Saudi Oil Minister had two choice words for Trump. "Not now."

31. Don't you wish you could remain as composed as Melania?

Melania's ABC interview "Being Melania" showed that she can remain calm and composed and thoughtful when asked those "tough" questions. Trump acts like a raving lunatic. He pouts and stiffens and talks fast, in choppy incoherent sentences. In his interview on 60 minutes, when asked a question he needed to evade, or could only answer with a lie, he fumed. He looked to the world like a mean, angry old man.

32. Can't you take responsibility for ANYthing?

Trump incessantly told his followers that the midterm elections were all about him. That they needed to get out and vote Republican, and that would be considered a vote for him. He has also said if the Republicans lose, he would not take any blame since he was not on the ticket.

33. Did you plan on toning down your rhetoric, as you promised, after a homegrown terrorist mailed pipe bombs to several Democratic officials?

Trump did read something from a teleprompter that sounded remotely like a change in rhetoric, but he read it with the same lack of spirit, empathy, and commitment he always displays whenever he's coerced into saying something in public he does not want to. But it wasn't long after the teleprompter speech before the real Trump came roaring back. Shortly after calling for unity in the wake of the attempted bombings, he took a shot at "globalists." Then when someone in the crowd chanted "lock him up" in reference to George Soros, Trump let go a noticeably sincere little chuckle, pointed into the crowd and chanted "lock him up" right back. George Soros was a victim of the bombing attempt.

When asked if he would tone down his rhetoric for the safety of the American people, Trump replied that he had already done so. Later, in what could be construed as a threat, he added, "Tone down, no. Could tone up."

Earlier, Trump had tweeted how this "bomb stuff" had been an inconvenience to him: "Republicans are doing so well in early voting, and at the polls, and now this 'Bomb' stuff happens, and the momentum greatly slows - news not talking politics. Very unfortunate, what is going on. Republicans go out and vote!"

About a week later, after the massacre at the Synagogue in Pittsburg, Trump again complained about the "bomb stuff" but added how annoyed he was at the Pittsburg shooter, for he too had apparently been careless with his timing of gunning down innocent people as they worshipped in their synagogue. Trump appeared to insinuate that the shooter should have known his actions might upset Trump's midterm election momentum.

34. *Did you have to make your big presidential visit to the Tree of Life Synagogue on the same day they buried their dead?*

Right after the deadliest attack against Jews in the history of America, where a gunman massacred eleven worshipers and shot up their synagogue, Trump defiantly displayed his ever-loving devotion to the NRA by insisting that gun laws had nothing to do with the violence. He added that the victims would have been much better off if they'd had armed guards at their synagogue. This callous comment angered many in the heavily democratic Pittsburg community. The locals have always seen Trump as divisive and a fondness for him has proven elusive there.

Most of the community members did not want Trump to visit at all. A group of Jewish leaders wrote an open letter to him, telling him he was not welcome in the city until he firmly denounced white nationalists. Tens of thousands of people signed that letter. But the local officials must have recognized that a United States President would *have* to come. Trump himself would want to make it at least appear that he was a half-way decent human being -- just before the midterm elections. Knowing a presidential visit would be inevitable, if not welcomed, the Mayor and several local officials made only one request of Trump: that he *not* come on the day of the burials. That he grant the community a time to mourn, a time free from politics, a time to start healing their raw wounds. Please, they begged, do not come on the *day of* the burials.

So, how did Trump respond?

Exactly as you'd expect. He visited on that *exact* day.

Being a spiritual person, the Rabbi from the Tree of Life, where the murders had occurred, appeared to welcome Trump. On the surface at least. But not one local official came to pick Trump up at the airport. Only an obligated member of the National Guard, along with his wife, showed up there.

Trump invited four Republican and Democratic congressional leaders to attend with him; they all declined, making excuses not to go.

Thousands of anti-Trump protestors lined the streets along Trump's route, giving him thumbs down or sticking out their middle fingers. One man with a baby in his arms held up a sign, "We didn't invite you here." Other signs read "Words Matter" and "President Hate is not welcome in our state." Trump had to have expected something like this; he'd insinuated himself into a place where he'd been told he wasn't welcome, and he did so on the ONE day the officials had specifically asked him NOT to come.

Why would Trump do that? Surely Shameless Svengali has more executive time (previously known as *downtime*) than any other president we've ever known! He yaps on the phone half the day and night, frequently checks social media and reportedly watches TV a *minimum* of four hours a day. He could have waited at least *one* day before insinuating himself into the lives of these distraught people!

Not so fast . . .

Not so fast . . .

Trump *was* busy around that time. Doing what he loves most. Standing before a crowd of admirers who'd been instructed to appear enthusiastic when Trump tells them an assortment of lies and scares them and rallies them to get out and vote Republican.

After all, what's more important? Rallying up the base, or showing respect for anguished people, still in shock from having just endured something so utterly horrendous and unthinkable?

In Trump's mind, there was never *any* real choice.

He made the trip he felt obliged to make, on the day that was most convenient for *him*. On the one day he didn't have a rally to attend. After he put in his required appearance in Pittsburg, starting the next day, he continued on with his scheduled rallies. He even informed his followers all about the *warm welcome* he received in Pittsburg.

There *was* an open letter to Trump, signed by members of the Pittsburg Jewish Community that had welcomed him to the city.

Tens of *thousands* had signed the letter asking Trump to stay away. How many people do you think signed the welcoming letter?

Forty!

And that was conceivably only because of Trump's unwavering support of Israel.

35. Do you expect us to believe you care about our men and women in the military?

Brent Taylor, 39, a Major in the Utah National Guard, and the Mayor of a Utah city, was killed in Afghanistan while helping to train Afghan defense forces. This apparent insider attack, which also wounded another service member, was at least the second such attack. Taylor, who was serving his fourth deployment, left behind a wife and seven children.

Trump's twitter feed was absent any mention of Mr. Taylor. While Trump endlessly tweeted about how fantastic every Republican running for office was, and how evil or stupid every Democrat running for office was, and how the crowds had welcomed him in Pittsburg, and how criminal "invaders" were coming to take over our country, there was not even one mention of these alarming incidents, or of our hero, Major Taylor.

36. Do you think -- even just a little -- that Judge Kavanaugh might have lied to the Judicial Committee in any part of his testimony on the sexual assault charges?

After Kavanaugh's testimony, Trump tweeted: "Judge Kavanaugh showed America exactly why I nominated him. His testimony was powerful, honest, and riveting. Democrats' *search and destroy* strategy is disgraceful, and this process has been a total sham and effort to delay, obstruct, and resist. The Senate must vote!"

This tweet had to leave a good portion of the country wondering: *Did Trump watch the same testimony as the rest of us?*

Kavanaugh opened by saying he had written his testimony the night before. Later, despite news organizations reporting he'd been watching Dr. Ford's testimony, Kavanaugh stated that he did not watch her testimony. The reason he gave was that he was too busy working on his statement -- you know, the one he'd said he'd written the night before. Kavanaugh also made a point of how his drinking with his friends back in the day was legal since the drinking age was eighteen. During some of the time in question Kavanaugh himself was only seventeen, and by the time he turned eighteen, they had raised the legal drinking age to twenty-one. So, if he had been drinking during those years, it had most definitely *not* been legal. Yet he'd made such a point of the legality of that, both on Fox News and during his testimony to the committee.

When asked questions that made him uncomfortable, Kavanaugh evaded answering. Instead, he kept reviving the litany of how accomplished he was, how hard he had worked, how he had been on the football team, how he had gone to church every Sunday, blah, blah, blah.

He also responded many times that all the "witnesses" had claimed the event never happened. Many of the witnesses *had* said that they didn't *remember* the event -- not that they were certain the event never happened. Having served as a United States Circuit Judge and as a staff lawyer for numerous offices of the Federal government, Kavanaugh would have recognized the difference. Most people, even those not steeped in the intricacies of the law, also found it to be just plain obvious.

Judge Kavanaugh also made a point of stating that his old friend Mark Judge, who had also been accused in the incident, had signed a legal statement (carrying legal penalties if he lied) stating that this never happened. Huh? Mr. Judge *had* released a statement, but it was only a few paragraphs long. And his attorney had signed it. Mark Judge would not have suffered *any* legal consequences if that statement had proven to be less than truthful. This was yet another legal distinction that a high-ranking judge such as Kavanaugh would have *easily* understood.

Kavanaugh also insisted that he never drank to such excess that he might have had a blackout. Numerous people from his past disputed those statements.

When asked if he would agree to an FBI investigation to clear his name, he continually stated that he would do whatever the committee asked of him, knowing full well that the Republican-led committee had no desire for an FBI investigation. When pressed on the issue, Kavanaugh sat stone-faced for a few moments before resuming his standard set of rehearsed responses. Senator Grassley had to come to his rescue; then Senator Graham put on a bombastic display of feigned outrage meant to distract from the fact that the judge's inability to give an honest reply had become overtly obvious.

Kavanaugh's final question, which included looking a Senator in the eye and swearing to God that he did not commit the deed he'd been accused of, seemed unbelievably theatrical. Even for the dramatics we're used to witnessing in politics these days, this demonstration was *way too far* over the top, especially when Kavanaugh ended by emphasizing that he was 100% sure he did not do this. He even repeated the 100% part -- clearly staged, and an attempt to one-up Dr. Ford's testimony that she was 100% certain it was Kavanaugh that *did* do this. But wait, Judge Kavanaugh never watched Dr. Ford's testimony. He was too busy working on the opening statement he'd finished writing the night before.

Wow! What a coincidence then! Ya think?

37. Since Kavanaugh was very combative and biased in his opening remarks in response to Dr. Ford's testimony, how could he be the right person to sit on the Supreme Court -- a place where cool heads, even tempers, and fair-mindedness are to reign?

Judge Kavanaugh was confrontational during his "rebuke" of Dr. Ford's testimony, which he claimed he hadn't watched. In his opening statement, he blamed the Democrats for a conspiracy against him and even stated that this entire affair was revenge from the Clintons. He accused the Democrats of raising money to block his appointment -- as if that (which happens all the time in politics) were some deep state plot. He neglected to mention that *his* Republican donors, in support of *his* appointment, outspent the Democrats by millions and *millions* of dollars.

Kavanaugh was outright nasty and mocking toward several Senators who questioned him. He even made a threat against those who were merely doing their jobs, vetting him for the position. "What goes around, comes around," Kavanaugh railed at them.

Should the President of the United States really be *praising* this out-of-control man? Should Trump have pushed so hard to get Kavanaugh on the Supreme Court, a job this man can hold for life, a position which demands he be dispassionate, balanced and unbiased?

38. **With sexual assault accusations having been made against your Supreme Court nominee, did you worry about what message this might have sent to women? Oh, wait, sorry -- you already answered that. Your response to a similar question at a press conference proved how concerned you are about the feelings of women. This was the response you gave -- to ease the minds of American women.**

"The same with the Russia investigation. They tried to convince people that I had something to do with Russia. There was no collusion. Think of it. I'm in Wisconsin. I'm in Michigan. I say, gee, we're not doing well. I won both those states. I'm not doing well. Let me call the Russians to does anybody really believe that? It's a con job. And I watch these guys, little Adam Schiff and all the guys. He takes a call from a Russian who turned out to be a faker. You know, he was a comedian or something. This is so-and-so calling for -- he took the call. Why is he taking a call from a Russian? Senator Warner took a call from a

Russian. He was a comedian or something. But he said we have pictures of President Trump -- where can I get them? If we ever did that, it would be a big deal. Yeah, it's a con job, and it's not a bad term. It's not a bad term at all."

39. There were some who found that answer a bit confusing. You must have been pleased when the reporter pressed again about your concerns for women so you could clarify your remarks. Here is that caring response from you.

"I'll tell you one thing I can say. I have had a lot of people talking about this to me with respect to what's happening. Because it's horrible I'm going to have to get other judges, and other Supreme Court judges. I could have a lot of Supreme Court judges, more than two. And when I called up Brett Kavanaugh, spoke to him and his family and told them that I chose them, they were so happy and so honored. It was as though -- I mean, the about biggest thing that's ever happened. And I understand that. US Supreme Court. I don't want to be in a position where people say 'No, thanks. No, thanks. I don't want to. You know, I spoke to somebody thirty-eight years ago, and it may not be good.'"

We thank you so much from the bottom of our hearts, for those kind reflections on women in this country. Your empathy knows no bounds.

40. At that same press conference, another reporter asked you what message you had for the young men of this country. What was that message? Never mind, we have your response on that right here too:

"It is a very good question. It is a big moment for our country because you have a man who is very outstanding, but he has very strong charges against him. Probably charges that nobody is going to be able to be -- to prove. So, I could have you chosen for a position, I could have you or you or you, anybody, and somebody could say things, and it has happened to me many times. Where false statements are made and, honestly, nobody knows who to believe. I could pick another Supreme Court judge, justice. I could pick another one, another one, another one.

"This could go on forever. Somebody could come and say, thirty years ago, twenty-five years ago, ten years ago, five years ago, he did a horrible thing to me. He did this, he did that, he did that. Honestly, it is a very dangerous period in our country, and it is being perpetrated by some very evil people. Some of them are Democrats, I must say because some of them know that this is just a game that they're playing. It is a con game. It is at the highest level. We're talking about the United States Supreme Court. This can go on forever. I can pick five other people.

"At a certain point, the people are going to say, 'no, thank you.' This is the most coveted job probably in the world. And you know what? I would honestly say because I interviewed great people for, he's great. But I interviewed other great people for this job. I could conceivably imagine going to one of them and saying, it is too bad what happened to this wonderful man, but I'm going to choose you number two. I want you to go. And I could conceivably be turned down by somebody that desperately wanted this job two months ago."

Our appreciation knows no bounds. You have certainly inspired young men across this fine country of ours. Don't you think it was exceptionally SAD, BAD that the conference ended abruptly just as a reporter gave you yet another opportunity to address the fine young men of this country? You did just sort of walk out on that opportunity.

41. That press conference you gave during the Kavanaugh confirmation was late in the afternoon. Could it be you didn't have a moment to give additional guidance to the young men of this country because you were in a rush to get back to your private room?

According to writer Michael Wolff, the President of the United States locks himself into his private room nearly every evening around 6:30. Adding a lock of his own to the door angered the Secret Service Staff. Even in an emergency, it would be a challenge for them to get to their President.

Reportedly, Trump lugs several cheeseburgers into his private lair -- something to munch on while watching his three televisions -- all tuned to news of him! Allegedly, he becomes infuriated if the cleaning staff touches his bedsheets. Heck, they're not even supposed to pick up the shirts he throws on the floor. According to Wolff, Trump has chastised the staff, declaring that if his shirts are on the floor, that is because he put them there and wants them there! Wolff explained that Trump is petrified of being poisoned and gets particularly angry if someone touches his toothbrush. Alone in the room, Trump is said to wolf down junk food, scrutinize the news, then call anyone who will listen, complaining about how the press treats him unfairly. He also is reportedly said to utilize this time to strategize our country's future with his rich, powerful buddies and his friends from Fox News.

42. After that press conference, you came up with a more specific message for young men: "It is a very scary time for young men in America, where you can be guilty of something you may not be guilty of." Do you think this message is more relevant today or was it more so back in 1989?

In 1989 five young black and Hispanic men were wrongfully convicted of raping, beating and leaving a woman jogger for dead in Central Park. Donald Trump led the charge against these young, innocent boys. Trump paid $85,000 for advertising space in New York's newspapers, including the paper he now refers to as "The Failing New York Times." Trump's headline heralded a request to "Bring Back the Death Penalty. Bring Back Our Police!" Trump then wrote and signed: "Mayor Koch has stated that hate and rancor should be removed from our hearts. I do not think so. I want to hate these muggers and murderers. They should be forced to suffer and, when they kill, they should be executed for their crimes. They must serve as examples so that others will think long and hard before committing a crime or an act of violence."

According to one of the accused men, Trump "was the fire starter", as "common citizens were being manipulated and swayed into believing that we were guilty." The defendants and their families received death threats after newspapers ran Trump's full-page ad. One of the defendant's lawyers argued that Trump's advertisements played a role in the conviction: "He poisoned the minds of many people who lived in New York City and who, rightfully, had a natural affinity for the victim." He added, "notwithstanding the jurors' assertions that they could be fair and impartial, some of them or their families, who naturally have influence, had to be affected by the inflammatory rhetoric in the ads."

After enduring prison, for between six and thirteen years each, DNA and other evidence cleared the men of all charges. Even then, Trump continued to rant on and on about their guilt. Protests erupted outside of Trump Tower with the rallying call, "Trump is a chump!"

What was Trump's response? Did he apologize? Trump responded, "I don't mind if they picket. I like pickets."

Even while campaigning for President (nearly three *decades* later) Trump *still* led the rallying call that these men were guilty. U.S. Senator John McCain said he felt Trump's responses were "outrageous statements about the innocent men in the Central Park Five case." He claimed it was one of the many reasons he withdrew his endorsement of Trump.

43. You gave a rare public apology -- of course, you stated that this apology was not from you personally. You apologized to Brett Kavanaugh on behalf of our nation, even though at least half the nation seems to think Kavanaugh should be the one doing the apologizing. Don't you think the men, whose reputations you helped destroy in 1989, deserve an apology as well? Didn't having their reputations destroyed and enduring years in jail cause them more pain and suffering than what you say Brett Kavanaugh, now a Supreme Court Justice, was "forced to endure?"

Trump issued this public statement to Brett Kavanaugh: "On behalf of our nation, I want to apologize to Brett and the entire Kavanaugh family for the terrible pain and suffering you have been forced to endure. You, sir, under historic scrutiny, were proven innocent."

No one *ever* proved that Kavanaugh was innocent. The investigation that might have proven something one way or another was so controlled, it couldn't possibly have uncovered the truth. The innocent young men Trump had so enthusiastically scandalized -- the ones who *had been proven* innocent -- are still waiting for their apologies.

44. Did you really give the FBI free rein to investigate Kavanaugh?

Trump declared, "The FBI, as you know, is all over talking to everybody, this could be a blessing in disguise. They have free rein. They're going to do whatever they have to do, whatever it is they do. They'll be doing things that we have never even thought of. And hopefully, at the conclusion, everything will be fine."

This is a statement that Donald Trump made about the FBI background investigation of Brett Kavanaugh in connection with sexual assault accusations made against the judge. Trump made this statement at nearly the same time it was being reported that, according to sources with direct knowledge, the White House was controlling the entire scope of the investigation. Sources said the FBI did not have permission to talk to one of the accusers. The FBI also was not permitted to confirm employment data with the supermarket where Mark Judge had been employed at the time of the alleged incident. Dr. Ford had stressed several times during her Senate Committee testimony that knowing when Judge had worked there could help her in narrowing down the time frame of when the incident she'd described had taken place.

The White House had given the FBI a list of witnesses they *could* contact. And Kavanaugh's drinking history would not be part of the investigation. The results of that alone could have potentially proven beyond a doubt that Kavanaugh lied to the committee, thus confirming he does not deserve to sit on the highest court in the land. Just for lying. And -- even more inconceivable -- the two main witnesses, Dr. Ford and Judge Kavanaugh, were not allowed to be interviewed. Dr. Ford's medical records, evidence pertinent to the investigation, could not be examined, nor were her witnesses allowed to be questioned.

White House spokesman Raj Shah threw more fuel on the fire when he claimed the Senate had set the parameters of the investigation and that the White House is "letting the FBI agents do what they are trained to do."

It's hard to back that one up when knowledgeable sources reported that White House Counsel, Don McGahn, worked with Senate Republicans to make sure the scope of the investigation was "as narrow as possible." McGahn wanted the Senate to confirm Kavanaugh almost more than anyone -- proving yet another blatant example of conflict of interest within the Trump Administration.

FBI agents focused their investigation on ONE night that Kavanaugh had marked on his calendar. (Kavanaugh acted as if a calendar from his adolescence proved he never committed sexual assault; the Republicans on the committee seemed destined to back up that ludicrous postulation.) After not uncovering evidence of wrongdoing on that *one* date, and interviewing a handful of witnesses, the FBI closed their "complete" investigation. Of the witnesses they did interview, one had already stated she didn't remember the incident, and the other had a clear motive to lie. Those who controlled the investigation knew this; they knew for certain that nothing new could surface from interviewing these "safe" witnesses.

Several other people came forward, claiming they had information in the case. They were either ignored or refused an interview. Dr. Ford, who had some difficulties narrowing down the exact date of the incident, could have been more specific if the FBI had helped to determine when Mark Judge worked at a particular store. Of course, they had not been permitted to do so. Dr. Ford also claimed she knew for a fact that the date that the FBI had so diligently investigated, the crux of their case, could *not* have been the date of the incident. She could have helped them clear that up right away and steered them closer, or even *to* the actual date of the incident -- if Trump's Administration had permitted the FBI to interview her. Which they no doubt would have done if allowed. So, we're left wondering: where was all this "free rein" that Trump swore he had granted the FBI?

45. Your Administration has ensured the American people that your tweets are official presidential statements. Couldn't that mean then that the FBI should have taken your tweet, about them having free rein in the Kavanaugh background investigation, as official instruction?

No way. The FBI must follow the instructions of the person on the front lines running the investigation. During the Kavanaugh investigation, that person was Don McGahn, who had personally fought for Kavanaugh's nomination.

46. Does that mean that the following tweet of yours is meaningless? Except to hopefully rally your base?

"NBC news incorrectly reported (as usual) that I was limiting the FBI investigation of Judge Kavanaugh, and witnesses, only to certain people. Actually, I want them to interview whoever they deem appropriate, at their discretion. Please correct your reporting!"

I'm afraid so. That tweet of yours might achieve its intended purpose of rallying some of your troops and further dividing us -- but it is deliberately misleading, blatantly false and overall a big fat nothing!

47. You swore that Brett Kavanaugh would be disqualified if he lied to the Senate Committee during questioning. Are you aware that there's compelling evidence he lied in his testimony about one of his accusers, Deborah Ramirez? Following your self-imposed standards, you should have disqualified him. Right?

Under oath, Kavanaugh told the Senate Judiciary Committee that the first time he heard of Ramirez's allegations against him was when the story broke in the New Yorker. And yet, text messages exist to the contrary. As far back as two months earlier, Kavanaugh had reached out to people he'd known during the time of the allegation and asked them to cover for him regarding that story (*which hadn't come out yet*). He'd also reached out to an old acquaintance to provide a photograph of him with Deborah Ramirez, taken at a wedding years after the alleged incident. Though Ramirez's friend has told the press that Ms. Ramirez was very uncomfortable at that wedding, and tried her hardest to avoid Kavanaugh, there is a picture of Kavanaugh and Ramirez together. Ms. Ramirez is broadly smiling. The Kavanaugh team used this as "proof" that Ms. Ramirez couldn't have been upset with Kavanaugh or afraid of him. The team neglected to mention that both Ramirez and Kavanaugh were in the *wedding party*.

You heard right -- that was a photo of the *wedding party*. Not a casual, relaxed reunion of old buddies, but a formal, forever snapshot in time of the wedding party. The happy couple would have expected Ramirez to smile. Strange how Kavanaugh had defense witnesses all lined up against the allegation, long before he'd even *heard* the story. Hmmmmm . . . Disqualifying *yet*?

The Committee threw up the usual stone walls and never presented this information to the FBI even though they said they would.

Hmmmmmmmm . . . anybody else sensing a deliberate cover up?

Realizing that appealing to the Committee was futile, one witness then tried to submit the evidence to the FBI herself; she never heard back from them.

But wait, wouldn't this be *just* the evidence that would *prove* that Kavanaugh was a liar -- something that would immediately disqualify him from sitting on the highest court in our land? Besides -- lying to the Senate Committee is a federal crime. Even if Kavanaugh is innocent of what he'd been accused of back in the day, should the fine citizens of our country welcome federal *criminals* onto our Supreme Court?

Witnesses offered their versions of Kavanaugh's coverup. Physical text messages proved they were telling the truth. Therefore, this would be the type of evidence that McGahn (with Trump's blessing) would *not* allow the FBI to investigate, the kind of evidence that could actually *prove* something.

But McGahn, backed by Kavanaugh's sponsors (groups Trump must keep happy to remain king) chose instead to base their mock FBI investigation on other "*real, hard evidence.*"

Like -- Kavanaugh's 1982 calendar!

Now we're talking!

We all have little doubt that if the *honorable* judge *had* sexually assaulted vulnerable young girls during his adolescence, he would have marched straight back to Mommy and Daddy's house and boldly seared the proof of his triumphs onto his calendar! Then all the world could see and examine such evidence, throughout his lifetime, if necessary.

And yet -- there weren't any such conquests marked on his evidentiary calendar, were there?

What more need we investigate?

Case closed!

Nomination confirmed!

48. Do you honestly believe Dr. Ford had forgotten the real identity of her attacker?

After Dr. Fords' testimony, Trump spread it around that she couldn't recall incidents of the attack, then added that she was probably assaulted but (since her memory was so faulty) she was mistaken about who committed the dirty deed. It couldn't have been Kavanaugh, Trump insisted. Trump made these "gentle" digs before he began blatantly accusing Dr. Ford of colluding with the Democrats.

Any expert on sexual assault could have informed Trump (and everyone else who was following the hearings) that it's common for the surrounding details and the aftermath of traumatic events to become blurred within the minds of trauma survivors. But they almost always vividly recall the essential, emotionally charged facts of the assault -- specifically the identity of the attacker.

Oh, wait, how *could* Trump have realized these facts? The Senate Committee blocked Christine Blasey-Ford's legal team from allowing an expert to testify, despite the team's repeated requests.

PERHAPS SOMEONE
WAS ... MISTAKEN?

49. So ... you said the Iranian President, Hassan Rouhani, requested to meet with you during the U.N. General Assembly -- but you blew him off? Did we get that right?

Iranian President Hassan Rouhani stated that he had no plans to meet Trump during his visit to New York, citing that the United States had employed only threats and sanctions against his country.

50. Did you also blow off the Canadian prime minister, Justin Trudeau, who also wanted a one-on-one meeting with you during the U.N. General Assembly?

Though Trump unequivocally contended that Prime Minister Trudeau requested to meet with him, Trudeau emphatically denied making the request.

51. At a press conference, you admitted that four, maybe five women had accused you of sexual assault. Did we hear that right?

Actually . . . twenty-one women have accused Trump of either sexual assault or inappropriate sexual behavior, including Trump's first wife. Ivana Trump later backpedaled (but why would she have lied about it initially)? One other woman also withdrew her accusation (because of death and rape threats). So, if you knock those two off the count, the number of accusers falls to a mere nineteen. Did Trump somehow *forget* to mention at least fourteen of his accusers?

52. During that same press conference, you stated that opponents paid women to come forward with these stories to hurt you? Is that right?

Not exactly, even though that's how Trump's friends at Fox news extensively reported it, without any proof. There is zero evidence to suggest that anyone paid Trump's accusers to come forward. However, money has been raised to help them with their lives and legal fees *after* they came forward. Whether donations to these women were based on political motives or a desire to see justice done cannot be determined.

There *was* one democratic activist who *did* try to get *legitimate victims* of Trump to come forward and offered them money. His efforts were unsuccessful.

The type of nefarious activity that Trump suggested is much more prevalent on his side of the aisle. Activists on the right offered $10,000, and all expenses paid to *anyone* who would come forward with details of *any* democratic congressional sexual harassment settlement.

The same partisan efforts had attempted to bring down Chuck Schumer, the Senate Democratic leader from New York. But they had to back away from that after Mr. Schumer referred the matter to the Capitol Hill police for a criminal investigation and it became clear that they were attempting to use a forged document against Schumer.

The accuser of Democratic Senator Al Franken of Minnesota, Leeann Tweeden, had appeared as a semi-regular guest on the Fox News Channel show hosted by Sean Hannity, Donald Trump's confidant and adviser.

Roger Stone, a former Trump political adviser, tweeted that it was Al Franken's "time in the barrel" hours before any charges had been made public. Mr. Stone admitted that he'd been tipped off by someone "within the Fox network" about the forthcoming allegations.

53. Is it true, as you've been swearing to us, that you did you not collude with Russia, plus you never had any business deals with or accepted any money from the Russians?

When asked during an interview whether Russian funds have flowed into his businesses and if Putin has leverage over him as a result, Trump replied: "Is that the theory? I haven't heard that at all. I mean I haven't heard that. But I have nothing to do with Russia, nothing to do, I never met Putin, I have nothing to do with Russia whatsoever."

Makes you wonder why Trump's son, Don Jr., once said in an interview about the Trump organization: "We see a lot of money *pouring* in from Russia."

54. Can you tell me who was confused about Nikki Haley's announcement last April?

Nikki Haley said on the air that the U.S. would soon impose additional sanctions on Russia. Donald Trump (never one to do anything that might offend Putin) reportedly flipped when he heard this. Larry Kudlow quickly emerged offering the explanation that Ms. Haley must have been momentarily confused. Haley shot back, "I don't get confused."

55. Were you less than truthful when you said your father only loaned you one million dollars to start your career?

If Trump has told us once, he's told us a gazillion times: "It has not been easy for me. I got a very, very small loan from my father many years ago. I built that into a massive empire." Trump also told us he'd paid all that money back.

Actually . . . Trump received what would have been the equivalent in today's money of $413 million from his father's real estate empire. His father had been such a good provider that Trump was a millionaire by the time he entered elementary school. And don't think he paid his father back very much.

Trump *did* build an empire after stiffing his father for countless millions. But Trump mismanaged those businesses and drove them into the ground until he had to declare bankruptcy. Along the way, Trump also stiffed or shorted countless employees and contractors -- hard-working people who had helped him build that empire. Not only wasn't Trump's father adequately repaid for the money he gifted his son, he frequently had to bail his boy out! Think about it! How could anyone mismanage *that* much money? Who could take *that* much money, especially while stiffing his employees -- and do such a lousy job he'd have to declare bankruptcy?

According to Timothy L. O'Brien, one of Trump's biographers, Trump swore to him back in 2004: "I had zero borrowings from the estate. I give you my *word*." But as O'Brien researched his book, "Trump Nation", he discovered that Trump *had* asked his siblings to bail him out. He needed another $30 million dollars to avoid bankruptcy. But Trump owed *billions* of dollars in bank loans on his condo buildings, casinos, hotels, and other properties. His siblings had little faith he would meet his debt. They did eventually bail him out but only after making him put up his future share of their father's estate as collateral.

O'Brien wrote about this and guess what? *Surprise, surprise* -- Trump sued the author for libel. The lawsuit proved not only to be unsuccessful and bogus -- but during litigation Trump *admitted* that his family had bailed him out.

Imagine that?

Despite inheriting and squandering privileges far beyond anything most of could even imagine in our wildest dreams, Trump is *still* lamenting: "My whole life really has been a no, and I fought through it."

Somebody, *please*, bring out the violins.

Better yet, fetch those razor blades!

Just what type of financial "no" could Trump have been referring to? Judging from the facts, it appears as if Trump's family members were the ones who did all the actual fighting for Trump's enterprises.

56. That horrible commercial you promoted before the elections to scare the crap out of everyone - - the one about that cop-killing immigrant - - you had said it was the Democrats who let this treacherous man into our country. Are you sure about that and do you have any regrets for promoting such a horrific campaign commercial?

Trump tweeted and supported a pre-election commercial that was in such poor taste, even Fox news, Trump's personal news station, yanked it from their playlist. The commercial highlights an immigrant cop-killer, who swore in court that if he had the opportunity, he'd love to kill MORE cops. Interspersed within the ad are various images of immigrants attempting to break into our country, then it turns to footage of Trump, who portrays himself as our almighty savior. The Shameless Svengali subliminally reinforces, so we can never forget, that *he* is the only one who can save us from the immigrants coming to "invade" our country. But the commercial doesn't stop there. It states that the Democrats are at fault; they are the ones who allowed this murdering savage into our country. The ad goes on to state that the only proven way to stop this invasion would be to vote Republican!

Wow, dramatic and convincing, *right*?

Nah!

Just another pack of lies from our Shameless Svengali, trying to get Republicans elected so he can keep on playing king.

One version of the ad linked the cop-killing immigrant to the caravan; this man had nothing to do with the caravan. Plus, Trump claimed the cop-killer was inside our borders *because* of the Democrats. Actually, Bill Clinton had *deported* him. This guy was deported several times but kept sneaking back into our country. Most notably, Trump's buddy, Sheriff Joe Arpaio once held this alien on drug charges.

Remember Joe Arpaio? The racist Sheriff that Trump had pardoned, remember -- the guy convicted of criminal contempt? Yeah, that one!

You wanna know what Arpaio did? Did he prosecute this invading criminal? Did he deport this murderous villain?

Nah!

Arpaio let the guy go. That's right -- the same immigrant in the video that Trump used to scare everyone and turn people against the Democrats for not protecting them, had been *released* into the community by none other than Trump's own buddy!

Vice President Mike Pence had once said about Arpaio that he is: "A great friend of this President, a tireless champion of strong borders and the rule of law."

A MARRIAGE MADE
IN HEAVEN

57. Despite how your wife might explain it, have you ever thought the odd message she wore on the back of her jacket had anything to do with you?

Melania visited a detention center in Texas, which housed some of the children separated from their parents by the Trump Administration's policies. This visit accomplished nothing, at least not anything that obviously helped the suffering children. After visiting the internment camps and thanking the staff, Melanie showed us few signs of genuine concern or compassion about the abduction and abuse of children and infants.

She was too caught up in playing games.

While heading on and off the plane, the First Lady donned a plain green jacket, certainly not in keeping with her usual fashion sense. That alone seemed odd, but to further aggravate the situation, plastered on the back of that jacket, in huge white letters for the entire world to gawk at, was the question, "I really don't care, do U?" Melania clearly displayed these words for the press to photograph while she boarded her plane, just after visiting the children in the detention center. Many of the children that Melania's husband had helped to kidnap from their parents were only infants. Officials had left several of these precious little ones alone to cry their eyes out on hard, cold cement floors.

Although Melania has complained that the press should focus more on what she *does* rather than on what she *wears*, she meant to send a message with this jacket. And a very confusing one at that. Melania's office issued a statement declaring that it was *just a jacket*, that it had no message at all. That statement would have us believe it was perfectly normal for a former model (one who is still extremely fashion conscious and wouldn't normally be caught dead in that outfit, and has also likely wanted to cash in on the fact that as First Lady she would be one of the world's most photographed women) just happened to think a casual jacket with zany scribbling on the back – *a heavy cargo jacket* -- was appropriately suited for the humid, 80-degree weather.

The statement from Melania's office also assumes we'd believe Melania thought donning this particular jacket, manufactured by the Spanish-owned company Zara, (which had been fined for immigrant child labor abuses) was the perfect choice for Melania to drape herself in after just visiting the immigrant children that her husband had thrown into cages.

Thank goodness we always have Donald Trump to clear up any confusion!

Trump claimed his wife wore the jacket to convey a message to the "Fake News" media because they don't treat her fairly. Melania soon publicly agreed with her husband, contradicting the statement her own office had issued.

Some of the people left baffled by all this have speculated that Melania had meant the jacket incident to be a secret message to her husband.

Most likely this was just another family-planned publicity stunt, meant to distract reporters and the country from thinking about those petrified infants that Trump had kidnapped and left alone on that cold, hard floor. *Did we forget about them already?*

Yeah, it might be uncomfortable to be reminded of that cold, hard floor, but try laying down on one sometime -- all alone -- in the dark -- inside a locked cage -- imagining you're an infant -- and you'd just been ripped from your mother's arms.

Whatever is the true, clandestine meaning behind Melania's implausible wardrobe choice on that shameful, blistering hot day, she pulled a contemptible stunt. Yet it seems to fit in perfectly with countless other Trump family antics.

We can all take away one solid impression at least: Melania *does not* care.

Do U?

58. Did you have any input into the outfit Melania wore to the presidential debate, held just days after the Access Hollywood tape became public?

Folks, if we haven't figured it out by now, the Trump family is a TEAM, a money-making association. They are using their positions of power to make big bucks -- at our expense. Nothing they do is accidental. They are playing with our minds. They are keeping us all talking and guessing and wondering what's going on, while they whittle away at the fabric of our society and democracy -- all while scoring big bucks for themselves. Trump and his wife may sleep in separate rooms, but make no mistake – they're solid *business* partners!

Remember Trump's famous words in that Access Hollywood tape? "When you're a star, they let you do it. You can do anything. Grab them by the pussy." Does anybody think it was a coincidence that days after that tape was released Melania showed up at the presidential debate wearing a Gucci blouse, which featured a prominent "pussy-bow" detail. Let's not forget this was also the debate where Trump paraded out the women who had accused Bill Clinton of sexual misconduct, so the blouse could have been meant to send a dual message.

All the better to tease you with, my dear.

The Trumps are having a rip-roaring time of it, screwing with our heads.

59. When you took office you made a big (albeit phony) show of how you were divesting yourself of all your business interests. Don't you think you should require Melania to divest herself of her business interests? Why is she still making money off pictures of Barron when he was very young?

Melania licenses off her own son's childhood pictures. At a hefty price. She stipulates, at least, that no one use them in a negative context.

60. Didn't your wife reveal the true goal of "The Family's" Trump Presidency, with the initial wording of her lawsuit?

After Donald Trump took office, Melania Trump filed a lawsuit. She charged that an outlet had published damaging and unfounded allegations -- such as she had once worked as an "elite escort." So far, so good, *right*? Misleading information like that would be detrimental to one's reputation. But the wording of Melania's lawsuit indicates she wasn't nearly as concerned about protecting her *reputation* as she was about protecting the *money* she planned on making off her husband's presidency. Her *$150 million* suit argued that Melania's *brand* had "lost significant value," and had impacted "major business opportunities" that were otherwise available to her.

The suit spelled it out even further: "Plaintiff had the unique, once-in-a-lifetime opportunity, as an extremely famous and well-known person, as well as a former professional model and brand spokesperson, and successful businesswoman, to launch a broad-based commercial brand in multiple product categories, each of which could have garnered multi-million dollar business relationships for a multi-year term during which Plaintiff is one of the most photographed women in the world. These product categories would have included, among other things, apparel, accessories, shoes, jewelry, cosmetics, hair care, skin care, and fragrance."

Wow!

People! Do we need the Trump Family to spell out their true motives any clearer?

I really don't care.

Do U?

61. If Melania wants the press to focus on what she's doing, rather than on what she's wearing, why does she wear costumes intended to seize attention?

Someone who displays a jacket in front of television cameras that states, "I Really Don't care, Do U?" in big blazon letters on her back, right after she's come from visiting kidnapped babies held prisoner in a detention facility, does not exactly appear overwhelmed with the arduous task of keeping her wardrobe under the radar.

Neither could it have been anything but a deliberate attention-grab when Melania strutted her stuff on the Giza plateau in Cairo, in front of the Sphinx. Using one of the great pyramids (the only remaining wonder of the ancient world) as her backdrop, Melania glided back and forth effortlessly across her "runway", proving once and for all she hasn't lost a beat since her amazing modeling days. Almost immediately after posing and strutting for the cameras, showcasing a bizarre and arguably inappropriate Gangsta-style outfit, Melania chastised the press for noticing what she was *wearing* as opposed to what she was *doing*.

Come on! What she was *doing* was modeling an outlandish, unsuitable outfit for the press, ensuring that they, and everyone else in the world, would soon have little choice but to gawk at the absurdity of it all!

62. It's evident that you, Mr. Trump, are extraordinarily jealous of President Obama. But is something going on in your psyche about Michelle Obama too, or is it Melania who's jealous of Michelle?

Some say the night President Obama ribbed Trump at the White House Correspondent's Dinner, Trump decided that no matter what, he would be President. Though Obama's jokes were harmless enough and deserved enough, Trump never forgot. Since becoming president, Trump has done everything in his power to destroy Obama's legacy. And every chance he gets, Trump compares himself to Obama, struggling to convince the world he is better, smarter, cleverer, etc. Clearer signs of jealousy do not exist, no matter how hard we might search.

But, *come on* -- do Donald and Melania feel they must compete with *Michelle* too? It started with Melania's speech at the Republican National Convention. Melania pulled it off with style and grace. But the next day, members of the public noticed *similarities* to a speech made by Michelle Obama. This may or may not have been intentional -- things like that happen all the time, but still, there were those striking *similarities*. Melania said she had written the speech by herself -- with as little help as possible -- but after those *similarities* reared their ugly heads, a speechwriter suddenly surfaced to shoulder the blame!

Hmmmmmm . . . .

Yes, it *could* be a coincidence too that Melania's "Be Best" campaign slogan sounds an awful lot like the slogan Michelle Obama initiated: "Be Better," (which actually sounds much better grammatically).

Coincidentally also, Melania's "Be Best" pamphlet, the core of her campaign, was nearly identical to a document that the Federal Trade Commission released in 2014 under the *Obama* Administration. To make matters worse, as Melania was rolling out her initiative, the White House cited a link on its website connecting readers to the document. It urged parents to read the booklet "Talking with Kids About Being Online," that *Melania* had written . . . with a little help from the Federal Trade Commission. The White House later changed the wording to indicate that Melania had just been *promoting* the information. Is it possible that the White House had initially been attempting to state that Melania had just written the introduction to the pamphlet?

Melania has come under criticism for being stiff when she does the *First Lady Thing* of visiting children. Images abound of Michelle, smiling with children, dancing with them, getting up close and personal, just being happy and relaxed around children. The press has examined and criticized Melania, mostly unfairly, for not appearing as natural in *her* encounters with children. Melania and

Michelle are two different people, with distinct personalities. Not everyone has to make a public display of being all touchy-feely with kids.

But yet, now -- *suddenly*, Melania seems to have all the same photographs of herself with children in her portfolio as Michelle had in hers! It almost seems as if Melania went to Africa mainly to bring back those images of herself -- surrounded by children, all happy and relaxed. Smiling. Dancing . . .

The photos look almost *uncannily* like Michelle's pictures, from when she visited children in Africa.

Deja vu all over again!

I'M NOT A SMART MAN

You promised us you would drain the swamp then hire only the best. Can you explain why the swamp, under your watch, is instead getting murkier every day? Countless people in your administration have been accused of or convicted of crimes. Your personal swamp is also filled with wife-beaters, liars, bullies, thieves, people who are not very nice, and people who are not qualified for their positions. It's doubtful that a swamp, murkier than yours, ever existed throughout American history. Certainly, none of us has ever witnessed anything this tainted in our lifetimes.

What steps are you taking to clean your own swamp, and to ensure us that you'll make better future choices? Please explain why you would hire ANY of the people listed below, which is just a TINY SAMPLING of those who need to be drained from your swamp.

63. Dr. Ben Carson, Secretary of Housing and Urban Development?

Dr. Carson himself informed us he was not qualified for his position. "Having me as a federal bureaucrat would be like a fish out of water, quite frankly," he once said. Carson has also told just about anyone who would listen about how, as a teenager, he would "go after people with rocks, and bricks, and baseball bats, and hammers."

He also stated: "And, of course, many people know the story when I was fourteen, and I tried to stab someone.

And, you know, fortunately ... my life has been changed. And I'm a very different person now."

Glad to hear it, but . . .

64. Andrew Puzder?

Trump had nominated this winner to be our Labor Secretary! Thank goodness someone stopped this nomination before the man got the position. Puzder is dead set against raising the minimum wage. He also wanted to automate fast food businesses, claiming robots were great compared to *humans*. He hired an undocumented, illegal immigrant to do his housework. (Looking out for American laborers, huh? What better choice for Labor Secretary?) And, just like so many of the men Trump enjoys cozying up to, Puzder's been accused of beating his wife. Gotta give Puzder credit though for being resourceful. When accused of beating his wife in their car, he had a ready explanation for why he'd been driving so erratically. He claimed he was merely driving drunk!

65. Jared Kushner, Senior Advisor to the President?

Jared has zero diplomatic experience, yet Trump gave him a big fat job as Presidential Advisor along with a gazillion challenging "assignments" -- including negotiating peace in the middle east. After decades of trying, even the finest, most experienced and accomplished negotiators could not accomplish *that* task.

Jared focuses on his own wealth and comfort more than he thinks about the good of our country or the American people. Though his real estate empire had earned several hundred million dollars a year, Kushner used every trick in the book to avoid paying his fair share of taxes. This sends a clear message to the American people that he preferred keeping all the money for himself. He would rather not give back even one penny for the good of the country, forcing working-class Americans to shoulder his wealth.

Senior Presidential Advisor material?

Kushner's father also worked hard to avoid paying taxes. The man did jail time on 18 counts of tax evasion, witness tampering and making illegal campaign donations. Keeping it all in the family, when Kushner's father's sister became a witness for the prosecution, Kushner's father hired a prostitute to seduce his own brother-in-law. They caught him "in the act" and videotaped everything. What better way to ensure revenge against your own sister for telling the truth?

Despite actions that would alienate most moral children, Jared looks up to his father -- as his mentor. The younger Kushner once said, "He's given me everything I have in terms of the skills and the training and taught me about being a man."

True, Jared does possess certain *skill sets*.

Together with his wife, Ivanka Trump, he earned more than $82 million in outside income during his first year as Senior Advisor to the President. This should have raised ethical and conflict-of-interest red flags -- blatant enough that any honorable administration would have found it necessary to examine these issues.

Guess that just hasn't happened . . . *yet?*

Jared Kushner once published a newspaper, *The New York Observer*. According to software developer and former Observer employee, Austin Smith, Jared had ordered him to delete several "critical" stories. Kushner insisted that Smith erase stories on the newspaper's website that seemed "critical of his commercial real estate colleagues." At least one of those stories would have shone a light on Jared's buddy -- one of the worst landlords in New York City!

Besides being unethical, this practice is a definite *no-no* in journalism. Kushner's mandated deletion of the truth was the real "fake news." Elizabeth Spiers, the former editor of the Observer, stated that she was not aware at the time that her boss (Kushner) was circumventing the editorial team and privately instructing the tech team to remove the articles. She stated that if she had known about it, she and Jared would have had "big problems," adding that Jared is "such a coward." Spiers stated that Jared had gone to Austin Smith, knowing that since Smith was not an editorial employee, he would have to remove those articles.

But of course, Jared promoted *The New York Observer*, highlighting the slogan: "Nothing Sacred But the Truth!"

In general, Jared isn't a very nice guy. Though quiet and "somewhat" peaceful-looking, he never forgets any wrongs done to him -- or to his family -- perceived or otherwise. Former Governor of New Jersey, Chris Christie, was the prosecutor who helped convict Jared's father. (Christie was the U.S. Attorney for New Jersey at that time and did what he'd been hired to do -- put bad guys away.) Christie also happened to be close to Donald Trump, and years later Christie was in line for a big position in the Trump Administration, possibly even Vice President. It's been reported that Jared not only ensured that did not happen, he also saw to it that Trump fired Christie from the transition team along with everyone Christie had placed on that team.

According to Internet registration records, Kushner and his wife set up a private family domain just before moving to Washington, when Kushner was preparing to take up a high-level job within the White House. He has, at times since, used a private e-mail associated with that account to conduct official White House business. Using personal accounts rather than a government address to traffic emails to other members of the White House bypasses the Presidential Records Act requirement. This requirement states that all documents related to the president's personal and political activities must be archived.

The FBI had already investigated Hillary Clinton for this same practice, yet Trump often speaks of re-opening that investigation or starting a new investigation into Clinton's emails. During Trump's campaign, he often led his "troops" with chants of "Lock Her Up!" -- referring to Clinton's e-mail "crimes". To this day that chant can still be heard echoing through the arenas at Trump rallies. You would think The President of the United States would have more important functions to tend to than rallying the crowds with this ceaseless chant. Not only is Trump still using this chant against Hillary to get his followers charged up, but Trump has also led the identical chants against "new" people.

If Trump genuinely desires to drain the swamp of the people who have committed the crimes that he suggested Hillary is guilty of, he should order the FBI to investigate Jared's e-mails. At least he should come clean with his supporters and inform them of Jared's indiscretions and change the chant to: "Lock HIM up." Let's have equal billing!

Besides double-dealing on his taxes, Kushner uses deceitful practices to ensure he gets what he wants out of life. That his actions worsen other lives along the way is of no consequence. Author Daniel Golden wrote that officials at Jared's high school were "dismayed" when Jared got accepted into Harvard. They claimed, "his GPA did not warrant it; his SAT scores did not warrant it." The same year that Jared applied to Harvard, his father donated $2.5 million to the university. Jared got in! Other students in Jared's class, many who were far more deserving according to school officials, did not make that sought-after final cut.

Besides all the cheating and double-dealing, Jared is also quite the vengeful person. He tried using his own newspaper to destroy people that had angered him. We all know about Kushner's ridiculous purchase of 666 5th Avenue in Manhattan, when he wanted to secure a posh skyscraper, a trophy building for his organization that could compete with Trump's buildings. Kushner paid far too much for the building (the most ever paid for an office tower in history) and afterward the Manhattan commercial real estate market crashed. Kushner was screwed. It got to a point where he couldn't make the payments on all the money he'd borrowed.

Enter Richard Mack, holder of a portion of the debt on that building. Kushner was allegedly furious when Mack wouldn't work with him on the terms of the mortgage. Though Kushner had gotten himself in over his head, he seemed convinced that he had a right to special favors. Mack didn't buy into it. He had his own investors to worry about -- besides he wasn't thrilled about the way the Kushners had been managing the building.

Kushner then told Elizabeth Spiers, the former editor of the Observer, to look into a potentially harmful story about Mack; he wanted it published in his paper. Spiers put her most aggressive reporter on the case, who came back with nothing. Insisting that there must be a negative story, Kushner directed Spiers to put another reporter on it.

That's where Foster Kamer came into the picture. He too investigated and found nothing. He claimed that by the time he'd made the third call on the matter he had discerned two very important facts: "1. The story was plainly bullshit. 2. Pursuing it wasn't a fool's errand so much as a goddamn moron's mission." Even after Kamer's reporting turned up zilch, Kushner still pursued the story, even setting up a meeting with himself, the two reporters, and the alleged source for this story. During the meeting, the source clammed up.

Foster Kamer reported that he asked Kushner why the source that Kushner had been certain would verify the story hadn't been able to confirm anything. According to Kamer, Kushner chuckled before replying: "Because he's not sleazy -- not like us, right?" Mack also claimed that he'd read that Kushner had ordered an *Observer* hit piece on the *The Star Ledger* -- the New Jersey newspaper that had helped uncover Kushner's father's corruption.

Even after Kushner left the Observer, the next editor-in-chief, a long-time friend of Kushner's, was still trying to drum up dirt on Richard Mack!

There have been numerous allegations and accusations that Kushner and his father have been trying to take advantage of Kushner's position in the White House by attempting to get funding for the son's failed building from various sources -- including businesses and other countries. Kushner has allegedly met with financial executives in the White House and hit them up for $500 million in loans.

Kushner's family offered "visas for investments" (in Kushner Company's luxury apartment complex) to Chinese investors at an event in China. Though the Trump Administration insists it wants to make it increasingly difficult for immigrants to enter this country, apparently the door is wide open to anyone willing to fork over half a million dollars to Kushner's failing company! Kushner's sister advertised her *connections* to Jared, to inspire investors to attend this promotional event. The Kushner Company banned reporters from the conference.

Kushner has also had high-level meetings with Chinese officials in which he discussed his family business. In part, this is why he couldn't get a full security clearance. US Intel worried the Chinese were using Kushner as an asset.

According to the New York Times, Kushner's company received an investment nearing $30 million from one of Israel's largest insurers. This happened just before Jared visited Israel with Trump and before Trump announced he'd be moving the American embassy to Jerusalem. Kushner also received at least four loans from one of Israel's largest banks -- a bank that just happens to be under criminal investigation by the US Department of Justice. Guess Jared's Middle East peace process doesn't look all that promising for the Palestinians? Americans should be petrified about how future terrorists are viewing this administration's shenanigans.

Jared's business also receives some decent influxes of money from various countries around the time Trump pays that country a visit. World leaders seem to be learning they are likely to procure favors from Donald Trump if they do something nice for the son-in-law.

Jared also snagged a $180 million business loan from a domestic company -- after he had spoken to that company's founder about a possible job in the administration.

All of Trump's magical *swamp-draining* antennas should be going up on this guy. Kushner is a man who doesn't play fair and more than likely Kushner plans on continuing to use his governmental position for personal gain. To stay true to his followers, Trump should order a full investigation on this guy.

Immediately!

Trump's own son-in-law is a prime example of someone Trump must drain from the swamp! Then again, might Trump make *exceptions*? Other than outside appearances, Trump and his son-in-law are very much the same. They both had fathers who were highly successful in real estate -- and both of those fathers had cheated their way to those successes.

Both Trump and Kushner will ruthlessly retaliate against any enemies, real or perceived. They love money above all else and, both being unethical, neither cares what they have to do to get it.

They each took their father's successful real estate businesses and, through their own imprudent choices and bad management, brought those businesses to, or to the brink of, bankruptcy. Trump and Kushner both travel the world with outstretched palms, to make up for their own business failures. Neither one of them cares that they had to sell their souls, or who they have to throw under the bus along the way, as long as they get their money. *And* their revenge!

Hmmmmm . . . sounds like another match made in heaven. And -- another swamp-draining exemption?

Jared seems like just the type of guy Trump would love welcoming into the family. Ivanka no doubt made her daddy proud the day she brought this man home.

Hmmmmm . . . wasn't there a theory going around that we choose spouses who are just like our parents?

66. Ivanka Trump, Donald Trump's daughter?

Without any qualifications to work in the White House, or any voters having put her there, Ivanka secured an office in the West Wing, along with a security clearance to receive classified information -- all this without even possessing an official title. Has Trump given her one yet? *Another* adviser? Ivanka appears to be more than a bit shady herself -- like she might also have been planning to use her position in the White House for personal gain.

After introducing her father at the Republican Convention, she tweeted about the dress she had worn -- one from her own line, which sold out in a day. Most of us witnessed Ivanka flashing her $10,800 bracelet when the Trump family appeared on *60 Minutes*. The next day her company promoted the bracelet to fashion writers, mentioning its appearance on *60 Minutes* and showcasing a photo from the interview.

The same night that Ivanka and Jared Kushner sat next to the President of China and his wife for dinner at Mar-a-Lago, the Chinese government granted Ivanka's company provisional approval for new trademarks. These trademarks gave her company monopoly rights to sell Ivanka's brand jewelry, bags, and spa services in China. Even though Ivanka had supposedly given up day-to-day operations of her businesses, she still owned them, and would reap the rewards once she left the White House.

Even after she surrendered her businesses, the Chinese Government continued to grant trademarks to companies associated with Ivanka and her father. Makes you wonder just how much the family is using present-day circumstances to set their future selves up to be sitting extra pretty?

The Chinese government floated a $500 million loan to a project partnered with the Trump Organization shortly before Trump announced plans to save the Chinese tech giant ZTE. Critics say Trump's plan risks compromising national security because some of that company's technology could be used to spy on American customers.

Shouldn't Trump be protecting us from intrusions from foreign governments? Americans should be outraged that Trump likely granted the Chinese *more* leverage to spy on us.

Not according to Trump! Not if it means more money pouring into his family coffers.

Criminal conflict of interest laws prohibit federal officials from taking part in government matters that could impact their own financial interests.

But that matters not inside the Trump Crime Family business. They write their own laws as they go along, to suit only themselves

The Commercial Bank of Dubai claims the diamonds from Ivanka's jewelry line are part of a $100 million money laundering operation. They are investigating Ivanka's now-defunct fine jewelry line.

When Donald Trump initiated the tariffs against China, he mysteriously left some items off his list. Those omissions were items that *Ivanka* manufactured.

Oh, lucky day!!

Along with her father and siblings Eric and Donald Jr., Ivanka is being sued by New York Attorney General Barbara Underwood alleging that the family used the private foundation for personal, business, and political expenses. The illegal activity allegedly took place for more than a decade which included: "extensive unlawful political coordination with the Trump presidential campaign, repeated and willful self-dealing transactions to benefit Mr. Trump's personal and business interests, and violations of basic legal obligations for non-profit foundations," according to the Attorney General's office.

The suit accuses the family of violating multiple counts of state and federal law. "Foundation funds were allegedly used to pay off Trump family legal obligations, promote Trump businesses, purchase personal items, and influence the president's 2016 campaign."

Ivanka has promoted a Trump Administration message that companies need to hire American. And yet -- her company manufactured most of its shoes, clothing, and handbags in China and Hong Kong. The Associated Press spoke with workers at a factory in Ganzhou, China that made Ivanka's shoes. Those workers described long hours, low pay and abuse.

Ivanka has also committed fraud. While working in her father's real estate company, she lied to prospective buyers about how many units in a building had been sold, how quickly they were selling, etc. An audiotape of her in the act has been uncovered. This is tangible evidence of her telling outright lies to prospective buyers, which is definitely fraud!

Ivanka gave up her businesses saying she wanted to focus on her work in Washington. There's nothing to stop her from going back to those businesses once her time in Washington is up. That she is still being granted trademarks from China shines a light on her intent.

Of course, she may also be planning on taking over Daddy's throne as our future queen!

In the meantime, it's clear that Ivanka is just the type of person that Trump promised us he would drain *from* the swamp, not add *to* the swamp. With direct evidence of her committing fraud, don't you think it would be more appropriate for her to be occupying a jail cell, rather than a coveted office in the West Wing of the *People's* House?

NOT A NICE GUY EITHER?

67. How do you reconcile touting yourself as someone who cares about workers when you stiffed your own employees?

Countless contractors have claimed that Donald Trump stiffed them. Just in the past three decades, Trump has been involved in nearly 4,000 lawsuits, many of them with ordinary working-class Americans. At least sixty of those suits involved people who claimed Trump, or his companies, owed them money and had refused to pay.

Documents show that, among *many* others, Trump failed to pay his dishwasher, a glass company, a carpet company, painters, plumbers, waiters, bartenders, real estate brokers, mechanics, subcontractors, installers and even many of the law firms that had represented him in these lawsuits.

Trump's companies have also been cited for numerous violations of the Fair Labor Standards Act. His businesses failed to pay overtime wages or even, at times, minimum wages. Trump's method for getting away with this crap was to tie the working man up in court for years. Trump knows he can outpower and outlast them. Lawsuits drain all the resources of working-class individuals if they go on too long. Especially if those involved in the lawsuits haven't been receiving regular paychecks. Many workers gave up or settled for much less than Trump owed them. They found out the hard way that, after legal fees, it can prove rather costly to sue Donald J. Trump.

Trump destroyed many of his former employee's lives. Honest, hard-working men and women ended up bankrupt after working for Trump. Family businesses that had been thriving for generations folded.

68. You claimed you hire only the best. If that's true -- how do you reconcile your slew of derogatory comments toward so many of your former workers?

During an interview, Trump and his daughter Ivanka made light of the lawsuits that so many of their former employees had brought against them. The Trumps stated that if they hadn't fully paid anyone it was because they didn't do a good job. If that were the case, it would mean that a huge portion of the workers that Trump hired did *not* do a good job. How could that be when Trump hires *only* the best?

Trump reinforced his position: "Let's say that they do a job that's not good, or a job that they didn't finish, or a job that was way late. I'll deduct from their contract, absolutely. That's what the country should be doing."

69. You stiffed your personal driver too?

Noel Cintron, Trump's personal driver for over twenty-five years, filed a lawsuit against the Trump Organization. According to the suit, Cintron accused Trump of failing to compensate him for about 3,300 hours of overtime pay. (He would have sued for a lot more, but the statute of limitations had run out.) Though Cintron claimed he averaged fifty-five hours per week, Trump didn't pay him the legally required overtime. Even when Trump had granted his driver a small raise, Trump induced him to surrender his health insurance, saving Trump much more money by not having to pay his driver's premiums.

As is always the case, the Trump organization denied any wrongdoing. Could it be that although Trump had used this man to drive him everywhere for *over a quarter of a century* -- placing his life in Cintron's hands -- Trump had felt that his personal driver hadn't done a good job? That's Trump's usual excuse for not paying his employees what they are due under the law. Mr. Cintron stated that Trump's non-payment was "an utterly callous display of unwarranted privilege and entitlement and without even a minimal sense of noblesse oblige."

70. Is it true you were not always very nice to your brother, Fred?

Trump talks about Fred often. He expresses how sad he is that his brother died of an alcohol addiction and explained that Fred's death had influenced him never to drink or smoke. But the evidence shows that the two brothers didn't exactly get along all that well. Donald Trump taunted his older brother about not being more involved in the family business. He made fun of his brother's chosen career as an airline pilot, comparing piloting a plane to the "lower-class" job of driving a bus.

71. Did you ever consider maybe just letting your son do some good in this world?

When Trump's son, Eric, started his foundation to raise money for a renowned pediatric cancer center (St. Jude Children's Research Hospital) the younger Trump showed good intentions. The Foundation held golf outings to raise money for the cause. Eric's fellow board members were close friends of his, and together they raised a sizable amount of money to help fight cancer in children. For several years, expenses for the golf outing remained reasonable, and it appeared most of the money was going to St. Jude -- where the donors expected it would.

But then -- Taaa Daaaaa!

Daddy Trump stepped in.

Things changed.

Trump Senior put members of *his* business organization on Eric's board. Eric's friends "resigned".

Huge chunks of donor money taken in at "Eric's" golf fundraisers were used to pay exorbitant rental fees for Donald Trump's golf courses. Eric's Foundation had been boasting about how much more of the donor's money was going to the actual cause, claiming usage fees at his father's golf course were being comped. That much promoted zero-cost advantage never existed, but at least the cost of renting the golf course was in line with what other foundations had paid to rent Trump courses.

But then, Donald Trump finagled a way to snatch money for himself -- by charging astronomical fees to his own son's foundation.

Charity experts stated that the listed expenses defied any reasonable cost justification for a one-day golf event, while donors believed every possible penny of their money went directly to the children. Not only that, the more the Foundation's website clarified that *all* the donations would help fight children's cancer, the less that turned out to be true.

For example, The Eric Trump Foundation made a $25,000 donation to the foundation of a Louisiana artist who created a portrait of Donald Trump for an auction at an Eric Trump Foundation event. Coincidentally, this artist's paintings frequently sold for around $25,000. An identical painting later showed up in a photo shoot, hanging above the couch in Eric Trump's house. His foundation would not respond to questions about the painting.

The Foundation has also made political donations and used foundation money to help settle one of Donald Trump's numerous business lawsuits.

The Foundation funneled more and more donations into various other charities -- without the donors having an inkling of this. Many of the people who ran these foundations (the recipients of donations from Eric's foundation) ended up spending big bucks at Donald Trump's golf courses. Trump also found a way to "launder" money directly through his son's charities. He would give a donation to Eric's foundation from his own foundation (money that others had donated) and through numerous clandestine methods (such as vastly overcharging for the use of his golf courses) Trump ensured that the money worked its way back into Donald Trump's organization. In other words, if you donated to Donald Trump's foundation, you were partly (or mostly) donating to Trump himself. And if you donated to Eric's foundation, you couldn't be sure *where* your money was going.

When asked to explain one such quizzical donation from his foundation, Eric Trump replied: "I don't know. I honestly don't."

NOT EVEN A LITTLE HEART?

72. Not Fred's children too?

It's been reported that Donald Trump eagerly stepped in to help his elderly, senile father rewrite his will. Supposedly, Trump and all of his siblings, and all of his sibling's *children* were in Trump's father's original will. But by the time Trump left his father's sickbed, his deceased brother Fred's children had mysteriously vanished from the will. How did Trump explain this? He insisted that his father did not want his dear brother Freddy's children in the will because he disliked Freddy's ex-wife.

73. Then you took it all out on a sick and helpless infant? Your dead brother's grandchild?

Trump's nephew, his brother Freddy's son, fathered a child who developed seizures, then contracted cerebral palsy. The Trump family agreed to pay the boy's medical bills. When Freddy's children sued for what they claimed should have been their share of the estate (the lawsuit claimed they were included in an earlier version of Donald's father's will) Trump retaliated by withdrawing all medical support for his nephew's infant son. This support was crucial for the child's well-being. Donald Trump explained why he withdrew all monetary support for his own brother's grandchild. Remember, this is the grandchild of the brother whom Donald proclaims to love and miss so very much. "I was angry because they sued," Trump proclaimed.

74. Don't you care at all about how you speak about other people or the places they call home?

At a meeting with Senators, Trump referred to Haiti, El Salvador, and African nations as "shithole countries." According to sources present, when discussing immigration Trump added, "Why do we need more Haitians, take them out." Trump also added that the United States needs more immigrants to come in from places like Norway.

75. Can't you ever stop bragging about yourself? Not even on September 11? Didn't you even care about workers in your own office building on that dreadful morning?

On September 11, 2001, reporters asked Trump in an audio interview if his building in downtown Manhattan (40 Wall Street) had sustained any damage. To the visual backdrop of the Twin Towers crumbling, viewers heard Trump's voice stating: "40 Wall street actually was the second-tallest building in downtown Manhattan, and it was actually before the World Trade Center the tallest, and then when they built the World Trade Center it became known as the second-tallest, and now it's the tallest."

What makes Trump's statement even more callous (as if that were possible) is that his remarks weren't even true. The destruction of the Twin Towers did not grant Trump's building the almighty status of being the tallest in Manhattan, despite how much Trump might have enjoyed bragging as such. On previous occasions, Trump had referred to 1 World Trade Center as "disgusting" and "a piece of junk."

76. Where's the money you pledged for 911 victims?

After the September 11th attacks, Trump pledged he would donate to the Twin Towers Fund for September 11th victims. Former New York City Mayor Rudolph Giuliani set the fund up " to benefit the families of firefighters and police officers who died in the attacks." Even though Giuliani (who happens to also be one of Trump's personal spokespeople these days) made one of his usual cryptic cover-up speeches for Trump, the fact remains that no record of Trump making such a donation has ever surfaced. And people have searched! Giuliani uttered something about how Trump had helped anonymously, but let's get real -- unless Trump forked over his "hard-earned" cash to Giuliani (highly unlikely) there is *always* a record *somewhere* of donations. Even anonymous ones. Even ones made in cash! Does anyone really believe that Trump could resist reporting a donation that might help him get a tax break? And if he had again used other people's money to make a donation, the Trump Foundation would have had to report it.

Years later, still without a trace of a Trump donation to the Twin Towers Fund, Trump's campaign officials came up with a new cover story. They suggested that Trump had donated to the Red Cross after September 11. No record of that supposed donation has ever been uncovered either. Millions of caring, working-class people opened their wallets after September 11. Many of them made donations they likely couldn't afford. But let's face facts: Our President, the "self-made billionaire," Donald J. Trump, despite repeated promises, never opened his burgeoning wallet for the families of those brave men and women who gave up their *lives* to save others on that dreadful day.

77. Did you ever plan on calling the two former U.S. presidents, Barack Obama and Bill Clinton, after they were targeted with pipe bombs?

Trump's actual response was: "If they wanted me to. But I think we'll probably pass."

YOU DON'T HONESTLY EXPECT US TO BELIEVE THAT?

78. Can you elaborate for us? Exactly what type of car do the Democrats plan on giving to all the immigrants after they lure them across the border?

Trump told us that Democrats entice immigrants into this country with promises of everything they'll ever need, including cars -- for free!

Wow! Sounds too good to pass up, right?

But did we hear Trump correctly when he hinted the Democrats could be giving each immigrant a *Rolls-Royce*?

Double Wow!

Whoever imagined Democrats were *that* well-heeled?

79. Did you actually expect we would believe that's not your voice on the Access Hollywood tape?

Trump offered us an apology, sort of, after the Access Hollywood tape (documenting Trump's total disrespect for women) became public. But the best that Trump managed to put forth was a disingenuous attempt at showing remorse -- peppered with excuses about "locker room talk." And we only got that half-baked apology, no doubt, after prodding from his advisers.

Trump later attempted to convince those around him that it wasn't *his* voice on that tape. Even though Trump had admitted that it *was* him speaking, he still tried later on to persuade people that someone had doctored the tape to make it *sound* like his voice.

No word yet if Trump tried to convince anyone that someone had doctored the visual portion of the incident. Perhaps that man filmed getting off the bus -- you know -- the dead ringer for Trump -- perhaps he was a Trump *impersonator*?

80. Did you really coin the phrase "Make America Great Again"? We'll just bet you thought that up all by your lonesome. Didn't ya?

Let's get this clarified once and for all. In Trump's own words: "The line of 'Make America Great Again,' the phrase, that was mine, I came up with it about a year ago, and I kept using it, and everybody's using it, they are all loving it. I don't know I guess I should copyright it, maybe I have copyrighted it."

WOW! Trump must be so exceptionally busy and in demand he can't even be certain if he'd taken the time to copyright that fantastic, unbelievably great line that he -- *and only he* -- came up with! Well, he'd better have his many minions (all of whom should have known better and taken care of this sooner) haul their asses straight down to the copyright office!

Once-in-a-lifetime opportunities like this must never go unheeded.

Trump has proven himself a mastermind in thinking up this slogan, and not only must he copyright it, the whole damn world needs to be made aware of Trump's creative genius! At once!

Except --

Except that --

When Trump tries to prove authenticity --

There's just one little -- *well maybe two little* -- hitches.

Ronald Reagan's campaign slogan was "Let's Make America Great Again."

And before Reagan, Hitler frequently spoke about the need to "Make Germany Great Again."

81. In some photos taken at your inauguration, it seems the crowd wasn't that sparse after all! Can you explain the differences in photos taken that day?

No need for Trump to explain. Through a Freedom of Information Act request to obtain a report from the Inspector General of the US Interior Department, the answers became clear:

On Trump's inauguration day, images sizzled across our television screens showing the attendance at the event looked rather sparse. The world observed that Trump could not draw the same large crowds that Obama had at his inauguration. This infuriated Trump, who endures a consistent, self-inflicted, one-sided competition with Obama.

In a rage, Trump himself called the head of the National Park Service and demanded new images. A government photographer rushed off to work on Trump's requests.

Trump sent out his White House Spokesperson, Sean Spicer, to berate the press for not reporting about the massive crowds at Trump's historic inauguration. Then Spicer falsely announced: "This was the largest audience to ever witness an inauguration! *Period*!"

Spicer had called the National Park Service several times that day requesting the "more flattering" pictures to back him up.

Following Trump's commands, The National Park Service cropped the pictures to cut out vast empty spaces. Crowd experts still ascertained that the actual attendance at Trump's inauguration was about one-third the amount of people who showed up for Obama.

82. Do you honestly get the biggest crowds at all your rallies?

Trump often boasts about how he fills the biggest stadiums at his rallies (which are *supposed* to be re-election campaigns for fellow Republicans). In reality, Trump's administration mostly books smaller venues, when larger ones are readily available.

DELUSIONAL

83. Do you still believe you know more than our Generals?

Donald Trump once said the Generals of the U.S. military were "embarrassing" to America. Trump has also claimed he knows more about ISIS than the Generals. Shortly before making *those* statements, he'd said he would rely on the Generals of the U.S. military to create a plan to defeat ISIS.

84. If you're smarter than all our Generals and all the great minds in Washington D.C., as you claim you are, what do you think about your ordinary followers? You know, the everyday working-class people who voted you into office?

That is a very good question, one many of us should be pondering.

85. Can you elaborate on your claim to know more about NATO than your Defense Secretary, James Mattis?

James Mattis is a retired U.S. Four-Star Marine General. From November 2007 to August 2010 he worked with NATO as the Supreme Allied Commander of Transformation. From 2008 to 2015 Trump busied himself hosting The Celebrity Apprentice and firing people on television. And yet, Trump now claims to know more about NATO than its former Supreme Allied Commander!

For real?

86. Do you honestly believe if Ivanka were not your daughter, you'd be dating her?

That is not only delusional, it's sick. But don't forget -- according to Stormy Daniels -- Trump told her (on the night of their sexual encounter) that she reminded him of his daughter Ivanka. And though Trump was once eager to get Daniels in the sack, now he refers to Daniels as "Horse Face." Ahhhh . . . the implications.

87. Is anyone who votes democratic REALLY tired of winning?

Trump stated at a rally that anyone who voted for a Democrat had to be really tired of winning.

This would almost be laughable.

If it wasn't so pathetic.

88. Do you honestly believe most African Americans find your rhetoric appealing?

At a recent rally, Trump called on blacks to "honor us" by voting Republican. As part of the same monologue, he talked about the Civil War and praised the Confederate General Robert E. Lee.

SCREWING THE AMERICAN PEOPLE

89. Just how involved were you in choosing the site of the new FBI Headquarters?

Okay, it's time to revamp the FBI's overcrowded and crumbling headquarters. Plans for the new building are all settled. The FBI headquarters will move to a nearby suburban campus. All the calculations are in and this move is the best way to solve space issues and please everyone. It's also the most cost-effective for the taxpayers.

All settled.

Right?

Not so fast . . .

Nothing is ever, *ever*, settled when The Shameless Svengali worms his way in . . .

Before becoming President, Trump had been interested in buying the FBI property -- perhaps to develop another of *his* hotels on the site. We all know how profitable his Washington D.C. hotel has been for him. Entourages of foreign dignitaries, all wanting special considerations and favors from the President, ensure Trump they stay at *his* hotels, and spend big bucks in *his* establishments.

Once Trump got involved, the plans to move the FBI out of Washington D.C. reversed course. Officials are now advocating a complete tear-down and rebuilding of the existing structure. Testimony about why this reversal occurred has proven inconsistent.

All this tearing down and rebuilding will cost taxpayers a fortune and won't even resolve the FBI's overcrowding issues.

So why the sudden change in plans?

Taaa . . . Dah . . . Enter -- Shameless Svengali!

If the selfish and narcistic Donald J. Trump can't expand *his* empire in a particular location, why would he allow *anyone* to develop there -- especially a possible competing hotel?

The White House denies Trump's involvement; it claims FBI leaders suddenly don't *want* to move anymore.

Is that a fact?

Ever notice how nearly *everyone* in Trump's castle changes their minds about *everything*, after a mesmerizing session or two with the Shameless Svengali?

Officials are even touting *revised* numbers, showing it would be more *expensive* to move. These fudged figures do not include money *from the sale* of the property -- a small fortune. Sources and documentation show that Trump attended several meetings about the fate of the FBI headquarters, and was dead set against the move from the start.

Ready for a little icing on the cake?

The Shameless Svengali put down his heavy-handed fist and informed everyone who attended any of those meetings, in no uncertain terms, that they were not to reveal *anything* that had taken place.

Ahhhh, thank goodness there are still a few "leakers" -- patriotic people who want the American people to know the truth about what goes on beyond Trump's castle doors!

90. Are you ever planning on showing the American people your tax returns?

Trump is the first president in nearly half a century who has not released his tax returns to the American people. His excuse during the campaign was that the IRS was auditing his returns and they wouldn't allow him to release them until they'd finished auditing.

Complete BS!

There is neither a law, an IRS ruling, or even a precedent that prohibits Trump from making his returns public.

As the Watergate investigation raged around him, Richard Nixon released his returns for public scrutiny -- *while* they were under audit. But Trump kept insisting it was the IRS that held him back from being transparent to the American people.

Campaign Trump promised the voters that once the IRS completed the audit, he'd release his returns. He tossed a few hints that this "might not" happen until after the elections, thus satisfying most of his supporters and alerting anyone who considered this a factor in their choice for the President of the United States.

The tactic worked.

So, what evasive methods did Trump use next? *After* he got elected?

The IRS *had* to have completed their inspection by then, but yet The Shameless Svengali still tossed around the phony audit excuse for a while. If Trump's taxes *were* still under audit, doesn't anybody wonder just how much misleading and potentially illegal information must be in them, for the IRS to scrutinize them so damn long?

There isn't an official law that says a presidential candidate *must* release his returns, but modern-day Americans expect transparency from a candidate for the highest job in the land. Anyway, when people asked Trump to release his returns after the election, the auditing excuse eventually morphed into a statement that the American people had no interest in seeing the returns.

What? No interest?

Numerous polls showed that 80 percent of Americans -- and 64 percent of Republicans -- *wanted* to see Trump's returns. That means most of Trump's supporters were waiting for him to deliver the promised goods. But Trump kept up the ruse that people weren't interested.

Eventually, even that got replaced with the mantra, "It's not going to happen." And, as Trump's Administration is adept at doing, they wore down reporters and the public with their repeated template answers. Then they went on the offense -- insinuating that reporters should be ashamed of themselves for asking. The facial and vocal expressions of Trump's spokespeople morphed from How *could* you ask? to How *dare* you ask?

The matter died down, just as Trump had plotted.

But The Shameless Svengali offered us *something* about his tax returns: "There's nothing to learn from them," he insisted.

Hmmmmmm . . . Then why can't *we* be the judge of that? Why not release the returns and help us stop believing there's an awful lot we *could* learn from them? For example, we might learn how little (if any) taxes Trump pays. Most of us realize by now that this "self-made billionaire" likely pays as little of his fair share of taxes as is humanly possible, so why not let us see if we might be wrong?

And then there's this: Though Trump's tax info wouldn't precisely reveal his net worth, it would give us great insight into his *actual* wealth. Numerous people have speculated that Trump isn't nearly as prosperous as he claims.

Trump also loves to brag about how much money he gives away. But Trump doesn't keep all the pledges or promises he makes. At a fundraiser for veteran's charities he claimed he had raised over $6 million for veterans. That turned out not to be true. Trump lied again, stating that he'd never said he had raised that money. Then he claimed he had already donated $1 million of his own money to veteran's charities. That also turned out not to be true. When asked what happened to the $6 million he had raised, Trump (who had denied raising the money after stating that he *had* raised it) claimed he had already spent it. That turned out to be -- *guess what* -- also not true.

Four months later, when a reporter asked what happened to Trump's $1 million donation, Trump stated that the groups he was donating to were still going through a long vetting process. That also turned out to be false since his campaign stated that they'd picked the donors four months earlier -- which means, they would have already vetted them all.

Trump did cut checks (after he'd been publicly shamed) and then, in Trump's usual fashion, he turned the situation around to make it look as if the reporters were at fault for asking where all this money he'd bragged about raising and donating had gone to. Trump lashed out, "Instead of being like, 'Thank you very much, Mr. Trump,' or 'Trump did a good job,' everyone's saying, 'Who got it, who got it, who got it?' And you make me look very bad. I have never received such bad publicity for doing such a good job."

Oh, our poor, poor king. Doesn't it make you want to race to the bathroom to get some tissues to cry into?

One check of Trump's tax returns would show all of his charitable donations and clear everything right up. Isn't that what Trump should want -- for reporters to see how honest and generous he *really* is, so they could tell him what a good job he's doing and stop trying to make him look bad?

The Shameless Svengali's returns could also show us just how much Trump's tax cuts benefit him personally. Experts say businesses like Trump's benefit more from Trump's recent tax overhaul than any others, even though Trump keeps insisting he is barely benefitting at all.

Poor dear . . .

Plus, we can get an indication of Trump's *international* financial dealings from his returns.

Now that could be a biggie! Something that Trump *really* might want to hide.

Nixon said it best when releasing his returns. "People have got to know whether or not their President is a crook. Well, I am not a crook."

When reporters asked the Trump campaign to comment on the fact that Nixon had released his returns while under audit, a Trump campaign spokesman clarified, "Mr. Trump is undergoing a routine audit."

Umhhhhh . . .

Huh?

91. How committed are you to working hard for the American people?

Some days our Shameless Svengali doesn't even show up for work until one in the afternoon.

Nice work if you can get it.

He watches from four to eight hours of TV every day. That's more time spent on watching television in *one day* than Trump spends on policy meetings for an *entire week*.

Trump's latest schedule shows he sometimes schedules as much as three times more downtime than work time. And what about the daily, essential Presidential Briefing? Umhhhhh?? Well -- maybe he'll attend that once or twice a week -- if he's feeling especially obligated -- or if the mood strikes, which it seldom does.

People in the *know* refer to Trump's down/personal time as "Executive Time." John Kelly had the bright idea to re-brand Trump's do-nothing time after Trump complained that he didn't have any time to himself to even think. A handful of aides still insist that Trump is working during this "Executive Time."

Okay, so how come during these "working" segments of the day, Trump's tweets generally surface?

And those tweets are all too often related to something that had just aired on Fox News, which would at the very least indicate that Trump is watching TV *and* tweeting during this -- *ahem* -- "Executive/Working Time."

Sad but true -- Trump skips most Presidential Briefings but spends hours absorbing himself in the "policies" that are being pushed by the Fox News team.

Let's lay this out now -- while pipe bombs were flowing through our mail system, and the deadliest attack ever against Jewish people in our country had just occurred, Trump was showing up for work around 1 PM or later. And the bulk of his "work" for those days was doing what he loves best. Rallying the "troops" at his conventions. Being the President of the United States has historically been one of the world's most regimented jobs. But not for Trump. In his mind he is *King*. And if the King wants to loll around on his throne half the day and night, watching the folks at Fox News say flattering things about him, who are we to begrudge him that "right"?

But never fear. If there's an excuse for a nighttime rally where friendly faces are likely to congregate, our King *will* emerge from his locked room and come to life to entertain the subjects! Such nights out also happen to stroke our King's ego.

A win, win for everyone!

The Shameless Svengali knows precisely how to incite his subjects and scare the crap out of as many people as possible -- all to ensure that they'll vote the way he wants and he can keep rolling his fat ass around on that throne of his.

Wouldn't we be way too selfish now, to ask that our King lower his ranking and actually perform any of the usual duties of the President of the United States?

DON'T FOOL WITH MOTHER NATURE

92. Do you realize that you did something good for sharks?

Finning sharks is a horrific practice. Butchers cut fins off the shark's bodies. Then they dump the rest of the shark (up to two tons of what then becomes a *waste product)* back into the ocean *alive.* The sharks can no longer swim without their fins, and when they can't swim, they can't breathe. They collapse to the ocean's bottom and are either eaten alive by other fish, or they bleed or suffocate to death -- or some combination of the above. The excruciatingly painful death always comes slowly.

All that waste and vile slaughter -- for one bowl of soup.

And what makes it even more coldhearted and cruel? Many consider shark fin soup a delicacy -- for special occasions. It's promoted as a healthy option, reserved for the privileged. But shark meat contains high levels of mercury, it's not at all good for us. Plus, people in the trade often treat the fins with harmful chemicals to make them look more colorful.

And the shark fin barely adds any flavor. It's placed into the broth solely to add *texture* to the gourmet soup that sometimes sells for up to $400 a bowl.

This horrendous practice brutalizes up to 100 *million* sharks each year. Sharks endure extreme agony, then sacrifice their entire lives, just so someone can have a little *texture* added to his bowl of soup. Other consumers might experience a few seconds of "importance" while being served this pricey broth in extravagant establishments.

Whoo wee! That's when you've just got to know you've hit the big time!

Does anyone want to venture a guess as to how Donald Trump feels about this pitiless practice?

Even though the brutal practice of shark finning has been illegal in our country since 2000, Trump regularly served shark fin soup in his casino restaurant.

Someone on Twitter wrote to Trump, imploring him to remove this item from the menu and Trump replied: "You like sharks?" Later Trump added, "Sorry folks, I'm just not a fan of sharks -- and don't worry, they will be around long after we are gone." Obviously, Trump never bothered to educate himself on the fact that conservationists are fighting to save sharks from extinction. Several species of sharks have already gone extinct from this brutal practice. Nor did Trump make himself aware of how much sharks suffer -- and for zero legitimate reason.

Either that or our Shameless Svengali doesn't give a shit!

Trump no doubt made amazing profits, pushing bowls of soup on the public at exorbitant prices. And once those dollar signs start flashing in Trump's eyes, he's incapable of seeing beyond them. Any misery inflicted upon another living being is of zero interest to him -- especially if Trump can slide a few more greenbacks into those bulging pockets of his.

Trump reportedly dined on shark fin soup with Vietnamese leaders in Hanoi. The Shameless Svengali is said to have kept slurping away, without comment, even while many of our legislatures are working hard to get our country out of the shark fin trade altogether.

The International Fund for Animal Welfare stated that by Trump eating the soup, he demonstrated that "he doesn't understand the plight of endangered species worldwide and is a signal to world leaders that the U.S. is abandoning its leadership role in global conservation."

Stormy Daniels claims to have first-hand knowledge of Trump's hatred for sharks. She stated that she witnessed Trump, engrossed in an episode of *Shark Week* while proclaiming, "I donate to all these charities, and I would never donate to any charity that helps sharks. I hope all the sharks die."

Geez, nobody asked him to *love* the sharks or go swimming with them, or even to throw a few bucks their way. But why *despise* them so much? Is this hatred for sharks what drove Trump to become a willing contributor to this horrific, agonizing practice?

Hmmmmm, maybe this is all just part of Trump's usual pattern -- of hating and lashing out at anyone or anything he deems more powerful than him.

Something for the mental health experts of this world to sort out!

After Stormy Daniels's shark story became public, donations poured in to organizations that help sharks. Many donations were in Donald Trump's name!

Though far from intentional, Trump may have actually helped a shark or two survive -- at least another day or two.

93. Who helped you doctor the misleading air pollution chart you put up on Twitter?

Trump posted a chart on Twitter, "proving" that America has the best air quality in the world. With his administration allowing big manufacturers and energy companies to pollute our air more than it already is, Trump must have thought this was a wise pre-midterm election move to stump us into thinking our air is fine.

First issue -- The Shameless Svengali's map is at least two years old; it couldn't possibly be a good indicator of all the extra crap that companies have released into our air since he took office. Second --Trump's map states that no people in the United States live in areas where they are exposed to air pollution concentrations above the World Health Organization's suggested level. Why then does a recent report from that organization state otherwise?

Also -- Trump's map, showing concentrations of "bad" air, includes DUST. So, areas of the world where there are a lot of deserts are showing the most concentration of "air pollution." The U.S. of A, that Trump refers to, doesn't have very many deserts. Therefore, we look better on the map.

In addition to all these other deceptions, Trump claimed our country has the best air in the world. We *are* doing better than many countries, but we do *not* have the best air in the world. More lies. The Shameless Svengali wants to make us believe the air we are breathing is fine and we need not take issue with his big-money friends polluting our air even further.

Trump neglected to post a chart that showed that in the United States, approximately 200,000 deaths occur annually due to air pollution. That number is only a drop in the bucket. Trump's policies are sure to make those numbers go waayyyyy up!

People who are dying early are losing about a decade of their lives thanks to polluted air. That's *ten whole years*! Can you imagine what you could do and accomplish with an extra *ten years* of life? But now that Trump and his team are in charge, we'd better prepare for the possibility of sacrificing at least *fifteen* years of our lives, so the rich can get richer. Anyone hear twenty? How about thirty years?

Going once, going twice . . .

The World Health Organization (WHO) issued a report that stated that 93% of the world's children, under the age of fifteen, breathe in air that is so polluted it puts their health at risk; air pollution is one of the leading threats to health in children under five. The WHO supports implementing policies such as switching to cleaner cooking and heating fuels, promoting cleaner transport, low-emission power generation, cleaner industrial technologies, and better municipal waste management.

What positive steps is Trump taking -- so that children world-wide don't get sick and die? Well -- whatever needs to be done, Trump is doing the exact *opposite*! NEVER FORGET, his already super-rich buddies want to make *more* money, and many of them can do this if Trump empowers their companies to pollute more! And that in turn allows them to contribute more to Trump's campaign -- so Trump can keep on pretending to be our king.

Is anyone detecting a pattern here?

94. The U.N. issued its most dire warning yet about climate change. What is your administration doing to help us avoid their predicted catastrophes?

The U.N. stated that climate change, left unchecked, would destroy the planet's coral reefs and cause increased droughts and wildfires that could spur massive food shortages. Limiting the effects of climate change to a more sustainable level would require "rapid, far-reaching and unprecedented changes in all aspects of society," including for human-caused carbon dioxide emissions to fall by 45% from 2010 levels by 2030.

How did Trump react?

After the report, Trump's administration prepared to make it *easier* for energy companies to release methane (one of the most powerful greenhouse gases) into the atmosphere. Methane routinely leaks from oil and gas wells. Trump's Environmental Protection Agency (EPA) will propose to weaken an Obama-era requirement that ensures that companies monitor and repair methane leaks. We also expect The Interior Department to release a ruling that repeals a restriction on the intentional venting and flaring/burning of methane.

White House Economic Advisor Larry Kudlow remarked that the U.N. report was "way, way too difficult."

Actually . . . the report wasn't difficult at all to comprehend -- not even for a child. Kudlow's inability to grasp the report's meaning is especially baffling since Kudlow must be "one of the best." Otherwise Trump (who promised to procure only the best minds) wouldn't have hired him. Campaign Trump would *never* hire a man who believes a clear and simple report is "way, WAY too difficult."

Right?

Trump's EPA also proposed weakening a rule on vehicle carbon dioxide pollution. They want to take away state's rights to govern their own controls on vehicle emissions. Didn't Trump claim his party is about giving power *back* to the states? Trump's EPA also wants to weaken the rule on carbon dioxide pollution from coal-fired power plants. They want to allow emissions to flow unchecked from smokestacks across this nation, from sea to shining sea.

When a reporter asked Trump about the scientists in his own administration who had warned of catastrophic climate change, he said, "You have to show me the scientists, because they have a very big political agenda."

Shortly after Trump's inauguration, the Administration deleted all mentions of climate change from the official White House website. The only reference that remained was Trump's vow to eliminate all of his predecessor's climate change policies.

And guess who got confirmed by the Senate to be the new head of the Justice Department's Environment and Natural Resources Division? Jeffrey Bossert Clark. You mean the climate change denier who defended BP in a lawsuit after the company released 200 million gallons of oil into the Gulf of Mexico? Yep. *That* guy.

The Trump Administration also disbanded its two panels of outside experts, who were there to advise the government on air pollution. These panels comprised two dozen researchers, from numerous fields, who reviewed scientific research and made recommendations on regulating specific pollutants. You guessed it though; these experts often encouraged the EPA to adopt *stricter* measures.

We can't have THAT! No, no, no -- absolutely not! But never fear. After Trump and his cronies tossed the experts out, they formed a brand-new committee, with alternative advisers. These new environmental "experts" are climate change deniers and people who have proven critical of stricter air quality standards.

Just the people Trump needs to justify his policies of polluting our world unchecked.

Trump responded to the U.N. report, saying: "I think something's happening, something's changing and it'll change back again. I don't think it's a hoax. I think there's probably a difference. But I don't know that it's manmade. I will say this. I don't wanna give trillions and trillions of dollars. I don't wanna lose millions and millions of jobs. I don't wanna be put at a disadvantage."

We all know the millions and millions of jobs part of Trump's statement is pure bullshit. And the trillions and trillions of dollars part is highly exaggerated. Besides, any money that organizations save by not enforcing crucial protections will go to the people who already control trillions and trillions of dollars, not to anyone who actually needs the money.

So, what's left in Trump's equation? Ummhh -- he doesn't want to be *put at a disadvantage*? Guess that translates to -- Trump would rather endanger countless homes and businesses, put wildlife at risk of destruction, mutilate Earth and gamble with *people's lives* rather than take the chance that *he* might "be put at a disadvantage."

Should we be counting on our President and his administration to help save our planet? Let's not hold our breath! Or maybe -- as long as Trump and his team of polluters maintain control -- we'd better get *used* to holding our breath.

95. What are you doing to protect wildlife?

The Trump Administration formed a wildlife advisory board called the International Wildlife Conservation Council. Sounds good so far, *right*? They'll want to protect animals, *right*?

Not exactly . . .

Trump didn't fill that council's board with the people who would be perfect and necessary for the job of steering policy on issues of wildlife preservation. Wildlife advocates and scientists would be the natural choice for these positions. But, oh no! Not in Trump's world. Trump filled his "Conservation" Council with rifle and bow manufacturers, celebrity hunters, at least one of Don Jr.'s hunting pals, and others who advocate the hunting of giraffes, elephants, and other threatened species.

Trump even put one of his NRA buddies on the board! Think, *sell more guns, sell more guns*! You can even chant it to the tune of: *lock her up!*

And let's not forget the Safari Club. They earned their seat at that table after they gave Ryan Zinke, the Interior Secretary who formed the council, a hefty campaign donation!

Let's keep it all in the family!

Comes a point when we have to wonder, just how stupid do these guys think Americans are? Even the most gullible amongst us must realize that a committee formed to *conserve* wildlife, being run by people just itching to *destroy* wildlife, makes the chances for any genuine conservation rather slim indeed. Yep, everyone on that board (that the Shameless Svengali wants us to believe protects our wildlife) has an avid personal or financial interest in killing animals. These blood-thirsty (*animal-preserving*) board members relish traveling across the globe, at great personal expense, just for the adventure of snuffing out the lives of innocent creatures. These animals never did them any harm. And yet -- there's just something about the orgasmic thrill that Trump's Wildlife Conservation Board members get while watching the life being sucked out of these majestic creatures. And knowing -- *they* did it!

Through their brave and herculean efforts -- *of pulling a trigger* -- they know that they took down the colossal, all-powerful beast!

Look, Mommy . . . I did that!

Some members of Trump's council might not share in those unbridled desires, but they sure as sin enjoy lining their pockets by helping others realize their passions.

The higher the stack of animal corpses -- the fatter the wallets.

Hunters pay tens of thousands of dollars for the "privilege" of destroying large, endangered animals. And they need guns and expensive equipment to achieve those goals.

Never fear! Plenty of fellow council members are right there to fulfill those needs!

To justify their *urges* to the segment of the population that can't quite contemplate their desire to kill for fun, these trophy hunters say that butchering the endangered animals is the perfect method for *conserving* them.

Okay, before this starts resembling a bashing of *all* hunters, please note that even though many Americans may not favor the concept of hunting and would much prefer exploring alternative methods of animal control, most Americans still understand that as of now, the practice has its societal function. This is *not* about local hunters who play by the rules.

This is about people who spend fortunes, jetting halfway across the world for a momentary thrill, and think nothing of bringing down a majestic animal that is on the world's endangered species list. It's about the hypocrisy of a sleazebag who would worm his way onto a board of presidential advisers under the pretense of being a conservationist, just to satisfy his urge to kill.

These are precisely the people who should NOT be on Trump's panel.

And yet, these are the exact people who make up Trump's wildlife conservation advisory team.

Even though Federal law *requires* government advisory panels to be balanced and uninfluenced by special interests, that didn't stop the Trump Administration from stacking the deck against the world's innocent creatures. Against all hope of us actually doing anything that might help these rare and wonderful, endangered animals. Trump's panel is only out to destroy; it has *nothing* to do with preserving.

Zak Smith, a senior attorney for Natural Resources Defense Council, said: "Elephants, rhinos, and lions face enough threats without the U.S. government giving the cover of credibility to trophy hunters peddling the self-serving notion that killing endangered species constitutes a legitimate strategy for conserving them."

But slaughtering these fine animals and posing proudly by their corpses is what Trump's *conservation* board members do. And *that* isn't even fulfilling enough for them. Trump's blood-thirsty pals need much more than mere photos of their "conquests." After the first few thousand showings, those two-dimensional images of animal corpses just fall flat! Besides, if they'll spend thousands and thousands of dollars to jet across the globe to extinguish one of God's majestic, defenseless creatures, don't you think they deserve to come back with something a little "meatier" than just a photograph? They're going to need something more substantial for the show-and-tell segment of their otherwise lily-white dinner parties. What they *really* expect is free rein to carve up the slaughtered carcasses, then jet back to America with bloodied suitcases full of choice body parts.

Who could ask for anything more?

There *had* been regulations in place, forbidding hunters from bringing back their "trophies" from abroad.

Those damn regulations all but ruined many a hunter's exquisite dinner party!

But never fear! Trump's Fish and Wildlife Service heard the cry of the hunters and granted their desires. The department lifted the bans on importation of these trophies.

Pure inspiration to any trophy hunter who might have been reluctant to travel across the globe at such a great personal expense just for the momentary thrill and a few pictures. Now they'll be much more eager to make the trek!

And slaughter countless additional majestic animals.

And spend extra, extra moola!

REAL conservationists predict that lifting the bans would add an unspeakable strain on the endangered species and all wildlife abroad.

But not so fast . . .Trump must have gotten wind that some of his followers might not be into all this grisly stuff. (Some of his buds over at Fox News actually disagreed with him on this issue too.)

Will wonders never cease?

And let's not forget -- Trump *needs* his followers -- needs them something awful so he can keep on playing king. And maybe -- *I said maybe* --Trump might actually have a trace of empathy somewhere, buried deep down inside that narcissistic soul of his. So, The Shameless Svengali did exactly what he always does. He made another useless, deceptive promise on Twitter to satisfy the followers who trust in his tweets, treat them as gospel, and rarely bother to check any further into what is *really* going on. Trump claimed he was holding off on lifting the ban -- that he had to review the situation. He even added, "Big-game trophy decision will be announced next week but will be very hard pressed to change my mind that this horror show in any way helps conservation of Elephants or any other animal."

WOW! For one instant -- *for just one instant in time* -- Americans thought maybe, just *maybe*, Trump would keep one of his major campaign promises. That he would stand up to the special interest groups, do what he might have felt in his heart was right, and start draining that swamp! Of course, he'd have to be draining the *new* D.C. swamp. The one of his own making, which is murkier than any in American history.

But alas, our preposterous, false hopes died in a flash. The council members were outraged at Trump's tweet. The NRA, which controls Trump, didn't like it one measly bit either. Yes, Zinke *pretended* to go along with Trump's outburst -- in public at least -- for a short while at least. But not long after Trump's tweet, Zinke began approving elephant and lion trophy imports -- on a case-by-case basis, of course -- to make it look as if there were *some* truth to Trump's tweet. In case anyone bothered to check. It's always best to provide The Shameless Svengali with some sort of cover, however transparent.

Trump, who could have stopped it all with one of his infamous orders, did nothing. Nothing at all. Thanks to Trump's silence, more majestic lions and elephants will fall. Their offspring will be orphaned. And drooling trophy hunters will carve the huge corpses to bits while their babies possibly watch from the shadows. Trump won't even lift a pinkie to save God's royal creatures. Despite the promises he'd made on Twitter -- the so-called official word of our president!

It doesn't take much of a stretch of the imagination to realize that in Zinke's "case by case" scenario, he will grant permission to *anyone* with enough connections, and/or wads of cash, to do whatever the hell they want to do to the helpless animals.

Which leaves us wondering . . .

Has Trump done anything *for* animals?

Well, for starters, his administration rolled back protections for endangered species. Environmentalists believe these actions will cause numerous species, some that have existed since long before Trump and his silver spoon ever made their appearance upon this Earth, to become extinct. Trump's upcoming budget proposal seeks to cut the species listing budget practically in half. His administration is also targeting the Endangered Species Act, a historic cornerstone of species protections in the United States. Imagine that: Animals that have called this Earth home for countless centuries, animals we *could* save, will soon no longer exist -- EVER AGAIN -- simply because Trump would rather shuffle what little money the government had allotted for protecting these animals off to his rich buds, so they can buy another yacht, or another diamond bracelet, or take another trip abroad to destroy yet another endangered animal and carve up its body and show off the head at their dinner parties.

Trump's Interior Department announced it was expanding access to hunting in at least thirty national wildlife refuges.

Trump's Fish and Wildlife Service (FWS) wants to weaken a rule that gives threatened species on private land the same protections as endangered species. This would strip threatened plants and animals of the safeguards our leaders have granted them for over four decades.

Trump officials informed FWS employees they could no longer advise land developers when they needed to apply for a special permit -- one that is necessary to maintain the habitats of endangered species. Officials further informed staff to let the *builders* decide whether they even *needed* a permit, even though the law mandates that those who might affect the natural habitats of endangered species must obtain that permit.

The Interior Department is easing restrictions that had limited access to certain critical wildlife habitats. Trump's Agriculture Department has withdrawn regulations that would have required higher production standards for organic livestock. Animal rights groups, consumers and organic farmers have condemned easing the animal welfare rule calling it "unconscionable" and "a travesty."

FWS withdrew regulatory actions to protect at least forty-two endangered species, including the green sea turtle and the yellow-billed cuckoo. Environmentalists agree this may have broken federal law.

Trump's team removed the Yellowstone grizzly bear population from the endangered species list. Trump is allowing hunters to take out baby bears and wolves in their dens. He is permitting the slaughter of wild horses for food.

But heck, all this blatant, senseless, thoughtless destruction of living beings makes more money for Trump and his already ultra-rich buds, and it helps keep Trump as King? *Right?*

You know it! Got to keep it all in perspective . . .

A leaked memo provided proof that the Trump Administration is attempting to hide its policies on endangered animals from the public. Could that be because 80 percent of Americans support the endangered species protections? *What they don't know won't hurt them, hey?* The Administration instructed FWS employees that they must be quiet about any changes to the Endangered Species Act. Policies and rules, briefing documents, and notes from decision meetings are being kept under wraps. And Trump really doesn't want the public to become aware of the countless times his administration overrode the advice of career scientists.

But Trump is methodically getting rid of all those workers anyway -- anyone who might see or hear too much and might want to "talk." If there are still any actual scientists left in any of Trump's Departments, who are desperately trying to make their cases, The Shameless Svengali will silence them as well.

DANGEROUS AND SCARY

96. Why weren't you at least as upset about Jamal Khashoggi (a United States resident and Wall Street Journal reporter) being assassinated at the hands of the Saudis, as you were about Nordstrom dropping your daughter's clothing line?

Our Shameless Svengali doesn't want a little thing like one man's brutal murder (especially a reporter who might not have always sung Trump's praises) to impede his business deals with the Saudis. Trump would rather dismiss the incident with a wave of his hand, informing us in no uncertain terms that Jamal Khashoggi wasn't even an American citizen. And we all know how Trump feels about people who "invade" our country. Trump considers people who live in the United States, but are not citizens, as squishable bugs under his shoe -- unless they happen to be sexy models he can grab by the pussy.

That the murdered journalist had skin that is darker than Trump's likely pushed the matter even further down Trump's agenda.

It looks as if the Saudi Crown Prince, Mohammed bin Salman, had his people lure the journalist to the Saudi consulate in Istanbul to have him murdered (and dismembered with a bone saw). But Trump seemed unphased about the gruesome incident, focusing instead on the *big arms deal* he claimed *he* made with the Saudis. He insisted that his interest was in American jobs, though he GREATLY exaggerated the amount of the deal and any possible benefit it might bring to American workers. Our Shameless Svengali was really doing what he does best: protecting himself and *his* business interests.

Trump said of the Saudi's, "I get along with all of them. They buy apartments from me. They spend $40 million, $50 million. Am I supposed to dislike them? I like them very much."

Trump's daughter, Ivanka, announced in a Middle Eastern publication, "We are looking at multiple opportunities in Abu Dhabi, in Qatar, in Saudi Arabia, so those are the areas where we are seeing the most interest." She added that although the company had not made any final decisions, "we have many very compelling deals in each of them."

"Having a President with global business ties means we've got ongoing worries that policy is going to be affected by his business interests," said Robert Weissman, president of Public Citizen, a nonprofit advocacy group.

Hmmmmm . . . even though there is solid evidence implicating Saudi Arabia in the September 11th attacks (not to mention that fifteen out of the nineteen September 11th hijackers were from Saudi Arabia) that country mysteriously does not appear on Trump's Muslim ban list. Why not? If Trump really wanted to protect us, Saudi Arabia should have been the first country on his Muslim ban list. Did he REALLY put that list together to protect us from terrorism? Or was it all just a show for Trump's followers? So that they would keep on believing he has their backs, and will keep him in office, and Trump can continue to play king while assisting his big business friends in the acts of raping and pillaging and ripping off our country! Plus, Trump can keep making big bucks off the Saudis.

Sound about right?

No way would Trump allow the slaughtering and dismembering of *any* number of animals, or *people*, get between him and his money!

Trump tweeted that he has no financial interests in Saudi Arabia. Even if that were true, Saudi Arabia sure spends an awful lot of money in Trump's establishments. Since taking office, the Trump Organization has benefitted from Saudi business at its hotels in Chicago, Washington, and New York. There has been speculation that the Saudi's even housed the Saudi Mission to the United Nations in Trump World Tower. Trump's hotel in Washington (where heads of numerous foreign governments meet and deposit big bucks into the coffers of the Trump Organization) received more than $270,000 from a Saudi Arabian lobbying firm.

Jared Kushner, Trump's son-in-law, also has close ties to Saudi Arabian Prince Mohammed bin Salman or MBS. Jared had cultivated a close friendship with MBS -- perhaps to use him to revive the Israeli-Palestinian peace talks? (Remember Trump claimed Jared would solve this issue for the world!)

More than likely, this blatant murder is a test by the Crown Prince to ensure himself that he has the Trump Administration in his back pocket. It's been reported that Kushner had been *giving up* people who'd been disloyal to the prince. The Saudis later imprisoned those same people and brutally tortured at least one of them, coercing him into signing over billions in personal assets to the Saudi government. Trump not only tweeted in favor of the Saudi Crown Prince after these barbaric treatments, but he also stated that the Saudis know "exactly what they are doing."

The Crown Prince even spread the word around about Jared's cooperation -- likely an effort to ensure the world of his hold over the Trump Administration. MBS reportedly bragged to the Emirati crown prince, amongst others, that he had Kushner "in his pocket."

Kushner has been in contact with the Crown Prince using Facebook's WhatsApp to communicate.

Lock him up! Lock him up!

Despite not having any political experience, Kushner took it upon himself to form these relationships with Saudi Arabia. Former Secretary of State, Rex Tillerson, along with H. R. McMaster, former National Security Advisor, expressed multiple concerns that Kushner was "freelancing U.S. foreign policy." Kushner (who couldn't even qualify for a full security clearance and was stripped of his top temporary clearance) apparently still reads classified information that his level of clearance does not permit. Trump lets him.

Trump and Kushner supported a Saudi Arabian led blockage aimed at weakening Qatar. Their help in blockading Qatar came shortly after that country failed to bail Kushner out of his nightmare real estate deal. Trump and Kushner also undermined Secretary Tillerson's attempts to mediate the crisis. Kushner did not even tell the Secretary of State of his conversations with the Saudi Prince.

The U.S. has very strong interests in Qatar, including an airbase where thousands of U.S. troops are stationed.

97. What precautions are you taking to keep our nation's top secrets . . . secret?

Despite Trump's supporters (who must be awfully bored with it by now) still echoing the chant -- *Lock Her Up* (concerning Hillary's use of a private e-mail server) the use of private communications and other dangerous practices is alive and well and even *flourishing* inside the Trump administration. Trump himself gave away highly sensitive intelligence to the Russians during a meeting in the oval office. Jared Kushner used a private app to converse with the Crown Prince of Saudi Arabia and allegedly talked about setting up backchannel communications with the Kremlin. This was during the presidential transition period. Before Trump was in office, before Kushner even held a position in the Administration, and without the knowledge of the U.S. Government. Plus, like Hillary Clinton, Kushner has used his private E-mail for governmental issues.

In Mar-a-Lago, Trump and his entourage spread classified documents about North Korea across their dining table -- in a very public place. Trump used a cell phone flashlight to read the documents better, thus broadcasting their contents to any hackers who'd been accessing his phone's camera.

The Chinese and the Russians consistently surveil Trump's cell phone, according to U.S. Intelligence officials. Enemies of our country are gaining much information about who Trump talks to and who he listens to (and who knows what else). This is all helpful information for them.

Despite repeated warnings that the enemy is spying on his personal phone, Trump continues to use it. The Presidential Records Act requires that all official presidential communications be collected and stored. But since when does Trump obey the law, much less some silly Presidential Act? Trump doesn't want the people he calls (to strategize and conspire with) to be logged in and become part of any public record. He uses his own phone and takes it with him everywhere. He even left it behind one day in his golf cart. *Nice place, the golf course, to make lots of private and financially beneficial, underhanded deals!*

Luckily for Americans, Trump can't be bothered with details of intelligence. In all likelihood, he doesn't even know much about military specifics or covert activities. So, simply because he's easily bored with the work of doing his job as President, he might not be spilling *too many* State secrets. But our enemies knowing who Trump talks to and what makes him tick is an exceedingly dangerous concept when it comes time for foreign governments to exert influence.

And Kushner has shown an avid and steady interest in the daily briefing of highly-confidential information. Although Kushner is not trustworthy enough to even obtain a full security clearance, Trump can let him read anything he wants. And often does . . .

You don't really think Kushner would jet off on secret trips to visit his buddy in Saudi Arabia and allegedly ask for money without bringing along something to offer in exchange, do you? It's not too much of a stretch to conclude that when Kushner sneaks off without informing anyone of his little trips, he's armed with many of our country's best-kept secrets in his little ol' back pocket!

98. *Didn't you denounce the reporting about your perilous use of personal cell phones? You stated that the report about your iPhone use was "sooooo wrong!"*

Trump protested the *New York Times* article about his cell phone use, stating that the piece was "long and boring." According to the Times (which stated that they sourced their reporting to several current and former White House officials) Trump uses three iPhones. The Times article further stated that Trump had been informed on numerous occasions that his cell phone calls are not secure. And yet Trump blatantly continues to use the devices.

Trump shot back that this report was so incorrect that he didn't have time to correct it. But -- no denying --

Trump *is* one amazing guy! Despite not having the time, Trump not only read the piece, he also commented on it. He trashed it and tweeted a sharp defense for himself. "I only use government phones and have only one seldom used government cell phone." A few hours later he finally broke free *again*, from whatever he'd been so busy with that had torn him away from Twitter. Again, Trump tweeted about the *New York Times* story -- perhaps he just hadn't been busy *enough* to get the article (from the newspaper that he invariably claims is failing) off of his mind? In the next tweet, Trump said the same stuff as before, but *emphasizing* how he *only* uses government authorized cell phones.

Whew! Sounds like the ultra-busy man got super-distracted from his busyness!

And to think -- someone might have actually believed the bull he tweeted about only using government phones.

If only . . .

If only he hadn't tweeted that defensive declaration -- *from his personal iPhone.*

99. Statistics show that domestic terrorists kill more Americans than jihadists. Do you have strategic plans in place to protect us from homegrown terrorists?

Nah!

Trump's got nothing in place to protect us from this burgeoning threat.

Zero. Nada. Zilch.

We *had* an anti-domestic terror program, which helped to fund organizations that helped fight domestic terrorism, but the Trump Administration did away with it.

100. How hard are you planning on protecting us from people like the recent pipe bomber?

Not at all. Trump expressed *annoyance* at the pipe bomber. But not even because the bomber could have killed countless innocent people -- oh no, not for any reason so trivial as that. If that bomber, an avid Trump supporter, had been just a tad more advanced in bomb-making, he could have killed or maimed not only countless Trump dissenters but also anyone who might have intercepted his packages along the way. But Trump doesn't give a damn about any of that. Hell no!

This "bomb thing" as Trump tweeted, broke Trump's campaigning momentum, and it happened just before the midterm elections, can you imagine *that*? The news outlets (in warning the public what to watch out for) had the *audacity* to report on the bomber! Poor Baby Trumpie lost precious air time. He didn't get the non-stop coverage he craves. And this was just when he was spouting his most vigorous hate and fear campaigns *ever*, against the "invading" caravan.

Poor, *poor* Baby Trump! How dare the "fake news" report on anything other than our Shameless Svengali? Remember, Trump needed all the news coverage he could get so that the Republicans could win in the midterms. So that Trump could keep on playing king. NOTHING else matters.

101. Just how deep in bed are you with the NRA?

Well, considering the NRA spent over $31 million making sure that Trump got elected, it's hard for him to be anything but the NRA's loyal lapdog, their roly-poly Trumpie Boy!

But how bad could that be, you might ask! Isn't the NRA just a group of sportsmen, banding together, exercising their second amendment rights?

WRONG!

The NRA may have started out innocently . . .

They *were* once an organization that served to unite sportsmen. The original group even zeroed in on the safe use of weapons. And, *shockingly*, the NRA used to advocate for safe gun regulations.

But those days and times vanished long ago down the barrels of the NRA's money-generating rifles. True, the NRA still keeps up a decent enough "front". Perhaps even enough so that (with its meetings and events) many of its members might not even realize that the organization has become little more than a front for gun manufacturers. But no matter how many memberships, or hats or tote bags the NRA sells, its members will never compete with the NRA's greatest contributors -- the ones with all the clout, the ones who now pull this country's political strings. They're the ones who *make* the guns. The guns that take so many of us down before our time -- like our beautiful, innocent children, our worshipers in synagogues and churches, and our fun-loving young people who might just be taking in a concert on an otherwise lovely evening. Gun manufacturers don't give a crap about any of them. They're interested in one thing and one thing only: selling *more* guns.

Yep, the heartless people who only want to sell more guns (no matter how many of us get shot up and slaughtered at concerts, in schools, or in churches, etc.) are the ones whispering (shouting, really) into our President's ear -- the ones calling all the *shots*.

Remember how Trump -- after the horrific school shooting in Parkland Florida -- had talked about making sweeping changes to the gun laws? How he claimed he would actually protect the people he's responsible for? Trump made a big show of it, even taunting that many of his Republican lawmakers feared the NRA.

Unlike himself, of course!

At that point, Trump might have been more afraid of the student survivors of that horrendous Florida school massacre who'd come to town to confront him. And Trump, being our Shameless Svengali, made all sorts of promises to those brave school kids -- promises he had zero expectation of keeping.

In direct defiance to the NRA, Trump declared that he wanted Congress to consider a complete ban on assault rifles. At the very least, he wanted to raise the legal purchasing age for these deadly weapons. He called for comprehensive gun control legislation, for expanding background checks for weapons purchased on the Internet and at gun shows, and for keeping guns out of the hands of the mentally ill.

Things felt *promising*.

At least until the grief-stricken students returned to school and the Shameless Svengali no longer had to worry about them staring in his face, peering through his devil mask.

And then, well, if we don't already know what happened next, we can surely guess. The NRA called their Trumpie Boy in for a little . . . *scolding*.

Now, why would you want to say or do any of that stuff? the NRA asked their Trumpie Boy. They may have even asked politely, *at first* -- before reminding him of that $31 million of theirs that had helped get him elected and of all the future campaign contributions he'd be flushing down the toilet if he didn't do exactly as told.

In the eyes of the NRA (and the gun manufacturers who hide behind the organization) even the loss of a few guns sales would mean less MONEY for them. And THAT, my friends, is a definite NO NO!

After the NRA called their puppy dog, Trumpie Boy, to task, Trump informed the world of his latest and greatest idea to save us: *We should arm teachers.*

Get it? Sell MORE guns! This would make gun manufactures even richer and happier. Trump would inherit an even fatter piece of the gun pie, just bulging with sweet bullets. And the NRA would continue to support Trump in his game of playing king.

Even though 80 percent of ALL Americans (including those who belong to the NRA) believe in some form of gun control, the NRA refuses to honor the wishes of Americans -- or even the desires of its own loyal members. The most avid hunters amongst us and the most passionate gun rights activists surely don't want to learn that some mad gunman slaughtered their children in school. But alas, though NRA members buy countless NRA hats and tees and love to attend those NRA events, they cannot compete with the influx of money that the organization receives from the gun manufacturers.

And these manufacturers know their roly-poly lap dog, Trumpie Boy, will do whatever they demand of him. Why else on earth would they invest over $30 million to ensure Trump got elected President?

"You have a true friend and champion in the White House," Trump once bragged to the NRA.

As if they didn't know . . .

As if they hadn't set it all up that way . . .

The NRA serves another purpose for gun manufacturers. The organization acts as their "front". They're the ones that everyone gets mad at after a horrific event. You don't hear people yelling about the evils of Smith and Wesson or see them protesting outside the factories of Heckler and Koch. No way! These guys cleverly set it up so that the NRA shields them from these sorts of *nuisances*. The trained public relations experts at the NRA take all the heat for them -- for a huge fee, of course.

The tobacco industry -- another group that has caused the senseless death of countless Americans through their greed and lies -- tried to create a similar organization to shield them from the public's wrath. Luckily for us that scheme did not succeed.

Besides all the NRA's obvious coverups, it also appears so much less "offensive" for politicians to take money from the NRA (it's a sporting club made up of ordinary people for heaven's sake) than for them to take money directly from gun manufacturers.

Shhhhh . . . let that be our little secret.

And, just as The Shameless Svengali keeps his followers in line with all his hocus pocus, mumbo jumbo, divide-and-conquer nonsense, the NRA warns its members that the left wants to take away *all* their guns. True, there are people in this world who wouldn't mind banishing every single gun from existence, but the main thing that most everyone wants – and the *only* outcome the left has *asked* for -- is gun *control*. They want legislation passed that would protect *all of us* from getting blown away by assault rifles. Which is -- the *exact* same thing that most "regular" members of the NRA want.

Gee! Who knew? We've all been so busy fighting and one-upping each other on social media (and elsewhere) we never even noticed that most of us want the exact same thing!

The policy of divide and conquer is alive and well, my friends -- Trump and the NRA, along with Trump's right-wing consortium, have been using it on all of us, and rather successfully at that!

Anyway, it should be clear to us all by now that no matter how much we Americans would love to protect ourselves from these horrendous mass shootings, we won't see any significant gun legislation in the foreseeable future. Not while Trump remains the "true friend and champion in the White House" to the people who manufacture and push guns on us. And we all know Trump will be nothing less *than* their true friend and champion if they help Trump to keep on playing king!

Never forget that nothing -- NOTHING -- EVER gets between Trump, his money or his throne. No matter how many hungry American children must make do with less food, no matter how many innocent men, women and children Trump causes to die in foreign lands through his indiscriminate bombing and ammunition sales to those who think nothing of the practice, no matter how many people in need of shelter end up living in tumbling down dwellings with rats and mold because the government won't maintain their buildings, no matter how many of our parks and open lands get sold to the highest bidders, no matter how many of us around the world suffer and die from poisoned water and air, no matter how many of us get burned alive or lose everything in fires sparked by climate change, no matter how many of us die or lose everything in hurricanes strengthened by climate change, and made even more catastrophic because Trump hijacked the money in our hurricane preparedness fund to house more immigrant families and infants in cages just to make his base think he has their backs, no matter how many of our precious animal species go extinct – *poof* -- *gone* -- *forever*, no matter how many of our elegant free-roaming, high-spirited horses get ground into meaty bits, no matter how many of God's gorgeous mammoth creatures get slaughtered and carved up for trophies, no matter how many reporters get brutally executed and dismembered with bone saws, no matter how many innocent Americans get gunned down in schools and places of worship, no matter how many of us get threatened with or killed by homegrown terrorism, no matter how many of us get murdered in the streets by emboldened elements of our society, and so on and so forth -- it does not matter. Money and Being King come first! Don't anyone EVER dare try to challenge that. That is Trump's be all, end all. The alpha and the omega. The all there is. The all there ever was. The all there ever can be.

NEVER, EVER forget it!

Roll over, Trumpie Boy!

Arf!

Disclaimer:

The "answers" to the questions in this book are based on a variety of news reports, along with the author's observations and opinionated views. The author took extreme care and diligence to provide accurate information but has not independently verified the reporting or writings used as sources of information. Therefore, in an abundance of caution, the author is not representing any of the information contained in this book as factually verified.

At the time of this writing, Donald J. Trump has not seen or been directly asked any of the specific questions contained within this book. His quotes, when provided as "answers" to these questions were based upon probable matches and (except for an excerpt from a news conference) were all used out of context.

Further, the author does not profess to know anyone mentioned in this book personally. Therefore, all mentions of motives or what someone might be thinking, or the reasoning behind what someone has done, etc. are being presented as pure conjecture and speculation on the author's part.

I hope you enjoyed this book and have gained some insights from the reading.

If you get a chance, I would definitely appreciate an online review.

It's extremely helpful to the author!

Thank you!!

You can find me on Twitter: @KACAuthor

Made in the USA
Lexington, KY
13 April 2019